ESSAYS IN INTERNATIONAL FINANCE

No. 161, December 1985

THE ROLE OF THE PARIS CLUB IN MANAGING DEBT PROBLEMS

ALEXIS RIEFFEL

INTERNATIONAL FINANCE SECTION
DEPARTMENT OF ECONOMICS
PRINCETON UNIVERSITY
Princeton, New Jersey

Library of Congress Cataloging-in-Publication Data

Rieffel, Alexis, 1941-
The role of the Paris Club in managing debt problems.

(Essays in international finance, ISSN 0071-142X ; no. 161, December 1985)
Bibliography: p.
1. Debt relief—Developing countries. 2. Debts, External—Developing countries. 3. Loans, Foreign—Developing countries. 4. International finance. I. Title. II. Series: Essays in international finance ; no. 161.
HG136.P7 no. 161 [HJ8899] 332'.042 s 85-23294
ISBN 0-88165-068-4 (pbk.) [336.3'435'091724]

Printed in the United States of America by Princeton University Press at Princeton, New Jersey.

International Standard Serial Number: 0071-142X

International Standard Book Number: 0-88165-068-4

Library of Congress Catalog Card Number: 85-23294

CONTENTS

The Role of the Paris Club in Managing Debt Problems

The world of economics and finance is full of mysteries. While many are genuine and arise from the complexity of human behavior, some appear artificially contrived by groups of players who find it convenient or advantageous to camouflage their activities from others. The Paris Club is a mystery of the second category, but less by design than by circumstance.

From 1978 to 1984, in a wave of debt crises that shattered confidence in the international financial system, twenty-nine countries appeared before the Paris Club to negotiate fifty-six debt-rescheduling agreements. Roughly $27 billion of debt-service obligations were deferred in these negotiations. Of necessity, the Paris Club assumed a more prominent role in the world of international finance, and important steps were taken to modernize its procedures.

Profiting from a greater willingness among the creditor countries to discuss the Paris Club in public, this essay begins with a general introduction in Section 1. In Sections 2 and 3 it reviews the basic principles and procedures of rescheduling negotiations in the Paris Club as they existed and were modified in the 1978-84 period, and in Section 4 it discusses the North-South dimension of debt.

The hallmarks of the Paris Club are its efficiency and its adaptability. Compared with these virtues, its shortcomings appear trivial. Nevertheless, the Paris Club is currently wrestling with two problems that are examined in some detail in Section 5. The first is prolonged recourse to debt relief through a succession of Paris Club agreements—a phenomenon described here as "serial rescheduling." The second is the emergence of debt-rescheduling arrangements imposed unilaterally by debtor countries, without negotiations with their creditors, that involve debt owed by private-sector borrowers—a phenomenon described here as "unilateral rescheduling."

Finally, Section 6 looks briefly at the role of the Paris Club in the Summit strategy for managing debt problems that was adopted in 1983.

Creditors and debtors understandably have a different appreciation of the Paris Club. From a creditor-country perspective, which is my viewpoint, the instinct is to conclude that the Paris Club has been tempered by the heat of the 1978-84 period and has emerged a stronger instrument in the service of the international financial community. For others who feel that the Paris Club

---

Special thanks are extended to Todd Crawford, of the Treasury Department, for his many valuable suggestions.

works against the interests of debtor countries, this essay may help to persuade them that the Paris Club is better than any alternative.

1 An Introduction to the Paris Club

The procedures for resolving an international debt crisis resemble a three-ring circus. In the center ring, the government of the debtor country negotiates with the International Monetary Fund to obtain a balance-of-payments loan in return for adopting a well-defined set of economic policies designed to eliminate its payments problem. In the second ring, the debtor government negotiates with creditor governments to lighten the burden of servicing outstanding debt and to obtain new financing. In the third ring, the debtor government negotiates with private creditors for debt relief and new financing.

Paris Club negotiations are part of the activity in the second ring. London Club negotiations with commercial banks take place in the third ring. There are close links among the activities in all three rings, but some basic distinctions separate them. Among the distinctions, perhaps the most important is that debt-rescheduling negotiations are organized from the perspective of the creditors, not the debtors. Credits from official institutions are discussed in the Paris Club regardless of whether the borrower is a public-sector or private-sector entity. Credits from commercial banks are discussed in the London Club, again regardless of the borrower's status.

Of course, it is not quite as simple as this. First, many credits from private lenders carry a guarantee of repayment provided by an official agency such as the U.S. Export-Import Bank, and credits to private-sector borrowers often carry a guarantee of repayment provided by the government of the debtor country. Forget the debtor-country guarantee: it does not influence where the credit is discussed. But a guarantee from an official creditor-country agency puts the credit on the Paris Club's platter. Second, credits extended by international lending institutions such as the World Bank are traditionally exempted from rescheduling. Third, nonbank private creditors (e.g., exporters or producers—or, more generally, "suppliers") have no established forum for negotiating a debt-relief arrangement. Fourth, commercial banks will generally discuss the provision of new credits in their London Club negotiations, but official creditors have made it a matter of principle not to discuss new credits in the Paris Club.

The spontaneous and informal character of many small circuses is also found in both the Paris Club and the London Club. Contrary to the impression conveyed by many journalists, and to the expectations of most countries experiencing their first debt crisis, neither club has a fixed membership or institutional structure. Each rescheduling negotiation with official creditors or commercial banks has an *ad hoc* character and can be considered a different "club."

In short, the Paris Club is not an international organization. It represents a set of *procedures* currently used for negotiating arrangements to defer payment obligations on credits extended or guaranteed by creditor-country government agencies to both public-sector and private-sector borrowers in debtor countries unable to meet fully their external debt obligations. The London Club represents the parallel set of procedures used for negotiating similar arrangements with respect to credits extended by commercial banks.

While neither "club" has members or a charter, their practices regarding participation are distinctive. In the Paris Club, the traditional participants (as creditors) are the governments of the major industrial countries of the West—generally speaking, the twenty-four members of the Organization for Economic Cooperation and Development (OECD). However, one of those countries (Turkey) has participated only as a debtor, and in any single rescheduling negotiation there are usually a dozen or more OECD countries that do not participate because they have not extended a significant amount of credit to the debtor country. Furthermore, other countries have participated as creditors, including Argentina, Israel, Mexico, and South Africa. In the London Club, the practice is simpler. All commercial banks that have any exposure to the debtor country participate. Smaller banks are represented by their countries' leading international lenders, which serve on a "steering committee" that negotiates with the debtor, but the negotiations are conducted on behalf of all banks.

The specific procedures of the Paris Club evolved gradually over almost thirty years. The first Paris Club rescheduling occurred in 1956 when Argentina agreed to meet in Paris with its official creditors to find a mutually acceptable basis for rescheduling payments due on officially supported export credits. Argentina returned twice, and Brazil, Chile, and Turkey together went to Paris five times in the late 1950s and early 1960s to obtain debt relief on obligations to governments, because the creditors had been overzealous in promoting exports to these rapidly modernizing countries. There were no parallel London Club negotiations, because commercial banks were not major creditors; the short-term trade credit that they did provide was not generally considered to have contributed to the countries' debt crises.

An aberration occurred in the late 1960s when creditor governments experimented with the use of debt relief as a form of development assistance. India and Pakistan, in particular, sought the rescheduling of aid loans to ease balance-of-payments strains. Several debt-rescheduling arrangements were negotiated, but these are not considered Paris Club agreements because neither country was in a position of "imminent default" and the granting of debt relief was not tied to IMF "conditionality." Again, commercial banks were not significant creditors and there were no London Club negotiations.

The debt-relief negotiations with Indonesia and Ghana in the early 1970s did qualify as Paris Club negotiations, even though the terms were highly concessional, because both countries were in default and had negotiated standby arrangements with the IMF. In each of these cases, external borrowing had mushroomed even as the productive capacity of the country's economy deteriorated. Debt relief on terms similar to those granted in the past would have imposed payment obligations exceeding the countries' ability to generate foreign exchange. Encouraged by political reversals which brought to power governments that were committed to developing market-oriented economies, the creditors granted Indonesia and Ghana exceptionally long repayment periods and favorable interest rates on the rescheduled debt. These cases illustrate the degree of flexibility possible in a Paris Club rescheduling, and they have been recalled with increasing frequency since 1981. Once again, commercial banks were not involved in either case because they were not significant creditors.

The mid-1970s constituted a period of transition. Commercial banks had to provide debt relief in an organized fashion for the first time (Zaire), and the London Club emerged as the standard rescheduling procedure for these creditors. Other noteworthy developments during this period were the first serious North-South negotiations on debt and the first signs of an epidemic of debt problems in Africa.

At the beginning of 1978, the Paris Club was a well-tested instrument with a respectable record; it had concluded twenty-six separate negotiations with twelve different countries over twenty-two years. The 1978-84 period tempered but did not change the instrument in any fundamental way, even though the Paris Club concluded more than twice as many agreements (fifty-six) in those seven years as in its first twenty-two. However, the frequency of rescheduling has not slackened, and some countries appear to have become dependent upon debt relief. Is there a basic flaw in the Paris Club approach? Would some of the alternative approaches proposed in recent years have been more effective? The discussion that follows answers "No" to both questions, but it points out several weaknesses in existing arrangements.[1]

2 Principles of the Paris Club

Imminent default, conditionality, and burden sharing are the three fundamental principles of Paris Club rescheduling. Additional principles, or "basic concepts," can be found in other accounts or in the UNCTAD resolution on

[1] A more comprehensive discussion of rescheduling cases in the 1975-83 period can be found in Brau, Williams, *et al*., 1983.

debt problems of developing countries adopted in 1980 (see section 4 below). They either follow logically from these three or are distinctly less important.

The First Principle: Imminent Default

Compared with devaluing or cutting back imports or diverting more local products to export markets, debt relief is an attractive option to a government facing balance-of-payments difficulties. Consequently, requests for debt relief are addressed to creditor countries with some frequency. The principle of imminent default is the main defense erected by creditors against capricious requests for debt relief. Creditor governments will not entertain a request for debt relief unless there is evidence that the debtor country will default on its external payments in the absence of such relief. The existence of substantial external payments arrears is generally regarded as sufficient evidence that the imminent-default criterion has been met.

Analytically, the test of imminent default is the existence of an *ex ante* financing gap. The techniques for measuring this gap improved considerably in the 1978-84 period and now form an important element in the preparation for Paris Club negotiations and the negotiations themselves. The starting point is usually the IMF's balance-of-payments projection for the debtor country for the coming year. The various components are rearranged in terms of sources and uses of foreign exchange. If projected uses exceed sources, this constitutes *prima facie* evidence that a situation of imminent default exists. Use of the IMF's projections avoids haggling over whether sources could be higher and uses lower, because the IMF's projections are deemed to reflect an objective assessment of the outlook in the context of the best politically feasible policy mix.

The accompanying table contains an example of a sources-uses calculation used by the U.S. government in preparation for the 1978 rescheduling negotiation with Peru. The individual items correspond to a projection found in the staff paper prepared for the IMF Executive Board describing the proposed standby arrangement with Peru. In contrast to the presentation normally used by the IMF, interest payments are grouped with principal payments rather than other current-account items, and both gross loan disbursements and repayments are shown rather than simply net disbursements. Also, where the creditors' estimates of disbursements and repayments diverge significantly, these are substituted for the estimates of the IMF. (Divergences occurred with disturbing frequency in the 1978-84 period.)

There was only one case in the 1978-84 period when debt relief was granted by official creditors in the absence of imminent default. The Pakistan rescheduling of 1981 was a throwback to the "aid" reschedulings of the late 1960s. During 1980, following the Soviet invasion of Afghanistan, Pakistan's Western creditors were anxious to strengthen Pakistan's stumbling economy.

Peru: Projected Sources and Uses of Foreign Exchange, 1979
(in millions of dollars)

	Sources	*Uses*
Exports	$2,380	. . .
Imports	. . .	$1,910
Investment income (excluding debt service)	10	130
Other nondebt services (net)	. . .	10
Transfers (net)	60	. . .
Loan disbursements	900	. . .
Investment (net)		20
Short-term capital, errors and omissions (net)	. . .	80
IMF (net)	10	. . .
Swap repayment		60
Reserve increase	. . .	180
	$3,360	$2,390
Balance before debt service	$ 970	. . .
Debt service:		
Bilateral official creditors:		
Principal		$ 335
Interest		200
Commercial banks:		
Principal		390
Interest		300
Multilateral and others		
Principal		315
Interest		60
		$1,600
Financial gap		$ 630

Note: The financial gap is more than closed by 90 percent relief on principal payments owed to bilateral official creditors and commercial banks.

Although some creditors were prepared to participate in a Paris Club negotiation despite the absence of a situation of imminent default, others (including the United States) argued successfully that a different "venue" should be found to preserve the integrity of the Paris Club process. The eventual solution was to negotiate debt relief in the framework of the World Bank–led aid consortium for Pakistan, which happened to be the forum used for the debt-relief negotiations with Pakistan in the late 1960s. The concern over the precedent created by this "political" use of debt relief is reflected in the fact that U.S. participation in the negotiations required a presidential decision.

The case of Peru can be used to illustrate some complications with the application of the principle of imminent default. Thanks partly to the individuals who happened to be representing creditor countries in Paris Club negotiations at the time, there was a spirit of experimentation early in the 1978-84 period. One of the notable innovations was to grant debt relief to Peru on two years of payments (1979 and 1980) rather than the standard one year. This was a contentious innovation, with opponents arguing that it would violate the principle of imminent default since there was some evidence that Peru would be able to meet all its payment obligations in the second year. The eventual compromise was to make the second year of relief conditional upon a subsequent standby arrangement with the IMF, in which an *ex ante* financing gap was identified for that year.

To the astonishment of many, Peru's balance-of-payments situation improved so dramatically during the course of 1979 that it decided to forego the relief offered for 1980 by both official and commercial-bank creditors. This is the only case of a country giving back debt relief granted in the Paris Club. One effect was to harden the position of those who had argued against a two-year rescheduling. Another effect was to leave the creditors with a singular fondness for Peru that manifested itself in an unusually generous rescheduling arrangement five years later. Unfortunately, the creditors' favorable predisposition toward Peru was not validated by Peru's performance under its 1983 Paris Club agreement.

The Second Principle: Conditionality

Having established the debtor country's need for debt relief, the creditors' next concern is to make sure that the country quickly regains its ability to service external debts fully and on schedule. Naturally, they begin by looking for the causes of the country's debt problem and asking that steps be taken to eliminate these causes.

This natural reaction was reinforced by the creditors' experience with debt rescheduling in the 1978-84 period. A major lesson learned was the importance of requiring the debtor country to implement a sound package of economic policies. The lesson is epitomized in the view that debt relief does not solve debt problems: good policies do.

At the beginning of the 1978-84 period, numerous creditor-country negotiators were inclined to believe that the debt problems being addressed were largely beyond the control of the debtor countries and would disappear once debt relief was granted on the appropriate terms. By the end of 1984, the opposite sentiment was equally prevalent: with the benefit of even the most generous rescheduling terms, certain debtor countries would probably remain uncreditworthy. The shift in mood, however, had remarkably little impact on the terms offered. The terms tended to reflect, more than anything else, the debtor country's ability to service debt in the next year or two and the creditors' desire to avoid precedents for more generous rescheduling terms.

The experience of the 1978-84 period also served to highlight a large contradiction at the heart of the Paris Club process. Creditors should reward far-reaching measures that lead to a rapid restoration of creditworthiness by offering more generous terms. Yet the stronger the corrective measures taken by a debtor country, the less relief is needed. Thus, creditors cannot reward good policies without violating the first principle. They cannot give relief that is not needed.

Creditors could negotiate with a debtor country to obtain the required policy reforms, but they have found a much simpler and politically safer device. As a precondition to Paris Club negotiations, the creditors insist that the debtor country conclude a standby arrangement with the International Monetary Fund.

IMF conditionality is absolutely central to the Paris Club process, because, more than any other factor, it determines the success or failure of the debt-relief operation. At the same time, it can be a weak point in the process, because the creditors are at the mercy of whatever accommodation is reached between the IMF and the debtor country.

The practical problem associated with obtaining conditionality by proxy through the IMF becomes a "chicken or egg" dilemma. Before concluding a standby arrangement with the debtor country, the IMF staff would like to know how much debt relief the creditors plan to provide so that it can assure the IMF Executive Board that the arrangement is viable, that is, that there will be no financing gap after allowing for debt relief and IMF drawings. The creditors, however, want to see the standby before they negotiate, because the policy commitments in the standby and the related balance-of-payment projections influence the amount of debt relief they are willing to offer.

This tug-of-war became acute in the 1978-84 period but was handled quite pragmatically in cases as different as those of Brazil (1983) and Sudan (1982-84).

In the case of Brazil, as with Mexico, the IMF played a major role in determining the amount of debt relief that would be required during the standby period. It was forced to do this because of the very large amounts of debt service due to commercial banks, the importance the banks attached to remaining current on interest payments, and the banks' reluctance to provide net new financing. The Fund managed its role successfully by consulting extensively with both official and private creditors during its negotiations with Brazil. In effect, the debt-relief terms were pre-negotiated via the IMF and were subsequently confirmed formally in the Paris and London Clubs.

In the case of the last three rescheduling agreements with Sudan, a different approach could be taken because commercial banks were not major creditors and official creditors have more flexibility than banks in rescheduling interest and extending new credits. To simplify a bit, the Fund staff negotiated standby's with Sudan and submitted them to the IMF Executive Board for *provisional* approval. The standby's did not go into effect (Sudan was unable to draw on the IMF) until negotiations with its creditors yielded a combination of debt relief and new money that eliminated the *ex ante* financing gaps specified in the standby's. These financing gaps were so large that even 100 percent debt relief (i.e., the deferral of all obligations, including interest payments) would have left sizable gaps. Since official creditors will not negotiate new money arrangements in the Paris Club, the IMF organized a special pledging session for balance-of-payments assistance to Sudan.

As noted above, the 1978 Paris Club agreement with Peru was for two years of debt relief, the second year linked to the conclusion of an IMF standby arrangement covering that year. "One-plus-one" agreements of this kind, with the IMF playing a key role, were subsequently negotiated with Togo, Turkey, Sudan, Sierra Leone, Zaire, and Liberia. (The 1980 agreement with Turkey was for three years; the others were for two.) With the exception of the Peruvian and Turkish agreements, all of these extended agreements broke down. The countries were either unable to conclude a follow-on IMF arrangement or quickly fell out of compliance with it. The creditors found themselves in a very awkward situation. Following the letter of the Paris Club agreements, the second year's relief should have been withdrawn. In each case, however, the debtor's balance-of-payments situation was very weak and there was no chance of getting paid what was due. These experiences soured the creditors on extended debt-relief agreements. Nevertheless, in response to a Summit-level political commitment, they concluded a "multi-year" rescheduling agreement with Ecuador in 1985. At the same time, considerable efforts were made to ensure that this agreement would be more successful than the extended arrangements negotiated in the 1978-81 period. The circumstances surrounding this case are discussed below in section 6.

Finally, in three cases IMF conditionality was not possible because the debtor countries were not members of the IMF: Poland, Cuba, and Mozambique. Since the creditors could not tie debt relief to an IMF standby, they negotiated directly with the debtors over policy reforms. In each case, a small task force of creditor-country experts was formed to visit the debtor country, evaluate the nature of its debt problem, and identify the measures to be taken to overcome it. The most difficult part of this process was trying to decide whether debt relief for these countries should be linked to meaningful reforms or to a set of quantitative "performance criteria" of the sort found in IMF standby agreements, such as the budget deficit, the exchange rate, the level of foreign borrowing, or the size of foreign-exchange reserves. In the end, the pragmatists prevailed, arguing that the statistical base was too weak or too easy to manipulate and that the traditional performance indicators were less meaningful in centrally planned economies. Thus these agreements conformed more to the form than the substance of the conditionality principle. There were occasionally intense negotiations over specific economic and financial targets, but without much expectation that the allocation of resources or the structure of incentives in the debtor country would change significantly.

The case of Poland was one of the most problematical for Paris Club creditors, especially because commercial banks negotiated rescheduling arrangements without any conditionality and left little foreign exchange for official creditors. Mozambique became a member of the IMF in September 1984, and it will therefore be possible for official creditors to obtain IMF conditionality in subsequent rounds of rescheduling in the Paris Club. Cuba stands out as the case in which the good faith of the debtor in undertaking reforms has been most in doubt, in spite of its good performance in meeting its revised debt-service schedule.

The Third Principle: Burden Sharing

The principle itself is simple: all creditors must provide relief that is commensurate with their exposure to the debtor country. The application of the principle, however, is one of the most complicated aspects of Paris Club negotiations.

There are four broad categories of creditor to consider, each one trying to get the best deal possible: (a) multilateral lending institutions, (b) official creditors participating in the Paris Club negotiations, (c) official creditors *not* participating in those negotiations, and (d) private creditors, notably commercial banks.

Multilateral lending institutions. As of the end of 1984, the multilateral lending institutions were the only category that had clearly established a preferential claim on the foreign-exchange resources of a country seeking debt relief. The category included the IMF, the World Bank, and the Asian, African, and Inter-American development banks, as well as certain other institutions such as the European Investment Bank and the OPEC Special Fund.

The arguments for exempting multilateral institutions from rescheduling are twofold. The first is that the debtor country as well as the creditor countries are members of the institutions and therefore both benefit from the exemption. The second is that the institutions bear their share of the burden of relief by continuing to lend to the debtor country.

To elaborate, the costs of multilateral lending are reduced for creditor-country members because, without the exemption, they would have to provide the multilateral institutions with more resources to maintain the same level of new lending. The costs are reduced for debtor-country members because the exemption is a key factor in maintaining the strong credit ratings that allow the multilateral development banks to issue bonds at favorable rates that are passed on to their borrowers. On the second point, analysis has confirmed that the major multilateral development banks have continued to be net contributors of funds to countries obtaining debt relief in the Paris Club, but that in certain cases the lesser institutions have not. (The IMF has also reduced its exposure in a number of cases; see section 5 on "Serial Rescheduling.")

In the light of the experience of the last six years, the only institution that seems to have a clear-cut case for virtually automatic exemption is the IMF. The monetary character of the Fund, the legal form taken by its lending (which is a purchase of foreign currencies with the debtor's own currency rather than a loan), and the role it plays in obtaining conditionality justify the preservation of its preferred status.

The preferred status of the other multilateral institutions may not be tenable indefinitely. In some countries, such as Tanzania, multilateral development lenders as a group account for the bulk of the external debt outstanding and the country's annual debt-service obligations. If one of these countries experiences critical debt-servicing difficulties and accumulates substantial arrears, it cannot be assumed that other creditors would "bail out" the multilateral lenders by providing new loans. It might also be hard for the institutions to justify a large increase in fast-disbursing nonproject loans to the debtor country when the purpose of the loans is so clear—to meet interest and principal payments on earlier loans by those same institutions. In such a situation, the institutions may decide to provide debt relief on terms similar to those offered by bilateral official creditors.

The question of which multilateral lending institutions should be exempted from rescheduling has generated some controversy. Obviously, the larger the number of creditors exempted in a particular case, the greater the burden on the creditors that do reschedule. After the IMF, the World Bank and the regional development banks seem to be on the strongest ground because the major creditor countries belong to all of them. To continue to exempt the European Investment Bank and the OPEC Special Fund, however, could make it possible for particular groups of creditors to escape participation in rescheduling by serving as a conduit for lending that would otherwise take place bilaterally.

An issue has recently emerged as a result of the World Bank's relatively new "co-financing" arrangements with commercial banks. Some of these arrangements come uncomfortably close to conferring on the World Bank's commercial partners its own preferred status in situations of default. None of the Bank's co-financing partners has yet been exempted from a rescheduling operation, but if and when this happens, it will almost certainly be against the advice of rescheduling experts in the creditor countries.

Participating official creditors. Despite twenty-eight years of Paris Club negotiations, debtor countries still have a strong tendency to seek bilateral relief before they accept a multilateral approach. They are often successful with creditor countries that do not belong to the OECD, but only rarely with OECD members. In view of the intense political pressures that can build up in some cases, the record of adherence to the multilateral Paris Club approach is remarkable.

Burden sharing among the creditor governments participating in a particular rescheduling operation is obviously the "raison d'être" of the Paris Club. However, it is much harder for governments to achieve equitable burden sharing than for commercial banks, because the governments' credits are extended on widely varying terms for a broad range of commercial, political, military, and humanitarian purposes. Therefore, the Paris Club creditors have opted for a simplistic approach. All credits extended prior to a specified date, regardless of their terms or purpose, are rescheduled with the same grace and repayment periods. At the same time, the interest rates on rescheduled debt are allowed to vary from creditor to creditor, with the general understanding that concessional credits will remain concessional and that penalty rates will not be charged.

The only serious burden-sharing issue that divided the leading Paris Club creditors during the 1978-84 period related to new credits. In several of the more recent cases (Sudan, Mexico, Brazil), official creditors had to provide new credits in addition to providing debt relief. No simple formula existed for determining how much each creditor country should contribute. Thus the pledging process was *ad hoc*, and the United States ended up providing more of the new money than it felt it should on burden-sharing grounds. To some extent, this outcome may have reflected the high visibility of the "new credits" problem in Brazil and Mexico—where the United States has traditionally had stronger economic attachments than other Paris Club creditors. (As noted earlier, new credits are not negotiated in the Paris Club.)

The IMF has been especially concerned about the difficulty of integrating new credits from official sources into the comprehensive packages of financial support organized for several debtor countries. Emergency "bridge" financing has been relatively easy to coordinate, because the leading contributors have been members of the Group of Ten, which is closely linked with the IMF through the General Arrangements to Borrow. Long-term development assistance has also been relatively easy to coordinate for countries such as

Sudan that have a World Bank–led consultative group. But some of the most important debtors, especially those in Latin America, do not have consultative groups and are more dependent on officially supported export credit than on development assistance. There have been preliminary discussions among representatives of the leading export-credit agencies about this problem, but so far no group has emerged to fill the gap and serve as a "partner" of the Paris Club in the process of managing debt problems.[2]

Nonparticipating official creditors. The technique by which Paris Club creditors achieve burden sharing with nonparticipating official creditors is to include a "nondiscrimination" clause in the standard rescheduling agreement. This clause commits the debtor country to obtaining equivalent debt relief from all its nonparticipating official creditors. If it accepts harder terms from any of them, then it is obligated to repay the Paris Club creditors more rapidly.

Even though as a matter of principle Paris Club negotiations are open to all governments that have extended credit to the debtor country, two main categories of official creditors do not generally participate in Paris Club negotiations: centrally planned countries and developing countries. The former do not participate presumably because they view the Paris Club as a "capitalist" process. They may also be reluctant to provide the detailed information on their credits that is traditionally exchanged among participants.

The nonparticipation of most developing-country creditors seems to be explained by different political considerations. Some stay away out of sympathy for the debtor country. They do not wish to associate themselves with the "onerous" Paris Club terms. Others feel they can escape rescheduling altogether or get more favorable terms by negotiating with the debtor bilaterally. Arab creditors, by contrast, tend to offer more generous terms than the Paris Club, perhaps because of Islamic sensitivities about usurious lending. The participating creditors recognize, however, that it would be harder to arrive at a consensus if more creditors with different philosophies participated.

Private creditors. Burden sharing with private creditors, notably commercial banks, has been the hottest issue in the Paris Club in recent years. The phrase "bailing out the banks" sums up the issue and hints at the degree of emotion involved.

Before 1970, official creditors could reschedule without worrying much about the banks. The amounts of bank lending were small, and debt problems were not associated in the public mind with "excessive" bank lending. By 1978, however, commercial banks were important lenders to most of the countries seeking debt relief from the Paris Club. The banks accepted the need to provide debt relief without much of a struggle, and the procedural

[2] Background on this aspect can be found in Brau and Puckahtikom (1985).

question was settled quite simply. The official creditors were not at all interested in bringing commercial banks into Paris Club negotiations, and the banks did not push to come in. The separate London Club evolved quite naturally, loosely modeling its approach on that of the Paris Club.

By contrast, the question of substance remains contentious. How much debt relief should banks provide to satisfy burden sharing? Reflecting fundamental differences between the purpose and terms of official credits on one hand and those of bank credits on the other, the concept of "comparable treatment" has evolved as the test of equitable burden sharing. When official creditors grant debt relief, the debtor country must agree to seek a measure of relief from banks that is as generous in the context of normal commercial lending as the relief offered by creditor governments in the context of their lending.

The difficulty with comparable treatment is that it is very hard to measure and harder to enforce. It is relatively easy to enforce when the banks refuse to provide any relief. This is what happened with Zaire in the 1976-79 period. Official creditors refused to provide further relief until Zaire obtained comparable debt relief from its commercial-bank creditors. And ultimately the banks agreed to provide relief.

At the other extreme, the terms Peru obtained in its 1978 agreements with the Paris and London Clubs were virtually indistinguishable. Furthermore, when Peru decided to forego the second year of relief it had obtained from the banks, it also had to pass up the second year offered by governments.

In most other cases, the terms of the Paris and London Club agreements were close enough so that official creditors did not feel they were "bailing out" the banks. In fact, in the case of Mexico the official creditors provided debt relief only to private-sector borrowers, while banks provided relief to both private-sector and public-sector borrowers. The cases where comparable treatment was hardest to achieve (or demonstrate) were those of Poland, Liberia, and Togo in the 1978-84 period, and Costa Rica and the Dominican Republic in the first half of 1985. Later in 1985, however, the problem of burden sharing by banks assumed major proportions when it became apparent that bank lending to the most important debtors had trickled to a halt. Ultimately, these concerns led to efforts to strengthen the five-point strategy discussed in section 6.

3 Paris Club Procedures

The Paris Club has one truly remarkable characteristic. It is capable of completing a rescheduling agreement involving billions of dollars of obligations in eight to twelve hours of negotiations at no cost to the debtor other than plane fare to Paris and two days' lodging for its delegation. The contrast with London Club negotiations is dramatic and certainly not lost on the debtors. The speed of Paris Club negotiations is due in part to the long experience of official creditors but probably more to the fact that a Paris Club agreement is an *ad referendum* framework agreement that is implemented by a separate bilateral agreement between the debtor country and each participating Paris Club creditor.

Since one of the purposes of this essay is to shed light on the mysteries of the Paris Club, it is necessary to survey briefly the steps leading up to a negotiation, the content of a negotiation, the main terms in an agreement, and the implementation process.[3]

Preliminaries

Rescheduling in the Paris Club is an unpleasant affair, and the official creditors must keep it unpleasant as an incentive to debtors to honor their debt-service obligations. Rescheduling is unpleasant primarily because it forces countries to take policy measures (in connection with their IMF standby arrangements) that imply a reduction of domestic consumption and slower economic growth. It is also unpleasant because the debtors are negotiating from a position of weakness and are rarely offered terms that appear generous to their citizens.

As debt problems emerge, debtor countries have only two alternatives to rescheduling. The first is to adopt far-reaching policy reforms that have the effect of sharply reducing import expenditures and boosting export earnings. In recent years, Korea and Indonesia are among the few countries that have followed this approach with success. The second is to seek more external financing. In 1978-84, this second alternative was attempted by many countries but rarely successfully. In some of these cases, the debtors quickly used up short-term lines of credit from commercial lenders. More often, they turned to creditor governments with whom they had strong political ties for extra balance-of-payments financing. For example, France has extended such financing to a number of its former African colonies, and the United States has extended it to Latin American countries such as Jamaica, Costa Rica, and Peru.

These cases are mentioned to point out that rescheduling is usually triggered not when the debtor country submits a formal request for negotiations in the Paris Club but when the official creditors decide they are unwilling to continue extending credit to the debtor country. The case of Israel could be used to illustrate this pattern. The level of assistance extended by the United States in fiscal year 1984 was explicitly linked to the level of debt-service payments due on U.S. military credits. If the United States discontinued its

[3] A more detailed discussion of Paris Club procedures can be found in Rieffel (1984).

large-scale financial assistance to Israel—even assuming a rapid turnaround in the performance of the Israeli economy—an Israeli request to the United States for debt relief would not be surprising.

Paris Club negotiations begin when the French government receives a debtor country's formal request for a meeting with the debtor's official creditors to negotiate a debt-relief agreement. If the debtor already has an IMF standby covering the period for which relief is requested, it will quickly be informed of suitable dates for such a meeting. Otherwise, the debtor is reminded of this precondition.

There is no particular mystery to the role of France in this process. To begin with, the French have a flair for negotiation. Furthermore, they are eager to offer their capital as a venue for every kind of international activity, and Paris is more centrally located than most other creditor capitals. In addition, the creditors are more comfortable with a host country that is a large creditor but not the largest, and the debtors are more comfortable with one that is known to be sympathetic to the Third World. Finally, and perhaps most important of all, after twenty-eight years of hosting such negotiations satisfactorily, any proposal to change the venue would probably be viewed by the French as a major affront.

Yet some negotiations held in Paris are not called Paris Club negotiations, and this is an example of French diplomatic skill. A number of debt-relief negotiations held in Paris between 1978 and 1984 were conducted "outside" the Paris Club for political or procedural reasons—generally because the creditors were not insisting upon the usual conditions, as was the case with Poland, which did not have an IMF standby, or because the debtor believed that a Paris Club rescheduling would tarnish its creditworthiness, as was the case with Mexico. In some of these cases, the negotiations were moved from the customary location, the International Conference Center on the Avenue Kléber. Nevertheless, they were chaired by a senior official from the French Treasury and followed standard Paris Club procedures. Generically, therefore, all these agreements (and all those described in this essay except the one with Pakistan in 1981) were Paris Club agreements.

In the final weeks before Paris Club negotiations begin, the creditors undertake intensive preparations. They examine the debtor country's request for relief, review the information produced by the IMF relating to its standby arrangement with the debtor country, and exchange information on the status of their credits to the debtor country. All too often in the 1978-84 period, it turned out that the IMF did not have comprehensive and consistent statistics on the debtor country's external debt when it negotiated the standby arrangement. In a few cases, the standby arrangement would have been significantly different if the statistics had been available. This is an important weakness in the Paris Club process that the creditors themselves can do little to correct. Only the IMF and the World Bank can achieve the desired breakthrough.

Normally, the World Bank has more information than the IMF on the external debt of a prospective Paris Club client. The reason is a matter of history. When the IMF was established, it did not envision playing a major role in debt-relief negotiations. By contrast, when the World Bank was established it required its borrowers to report regularly and in detail on their external public-sector debt. A few years later, it began to provide technical assistance to borrowers for establishing debt-reporting systems and to examine the borrowing strategies of borrowers during its periodic reviews of their development programs.

Unfortunately, when the number of debt problems mushroomed after 1976, the World Bank did not scale up its work in the debt area. And, because the World Bank had such a headstart, the IMF hesitated to duplicate the effort. As a consequence, the Fund currently relies heavily on the World Bank in the early stages of a debt crisis, although the information available from the World Bank tends to be a couple of years out of date. Through subsequent stages of a debt crisis, the World Bank seems to struggle to keep up with the Fund's information on debt without ever quite succeeding.

One logical solution to this problem would be to transfer the debt-statistics function from the World Bank to the IMF, but such changes are much easier to propose than bring about.

The Negotiations

Until the end of 1983, it was standard practice in the Paris Club to allow two full days for a rescheduling negotiation. Subsequently, the number of countries requesting debt relief became so large that the negotiations were sometimes reduced to a single day. In fact, the record for speed—about one hour—was set in October 1983 by Malawi, which had made a prior visit to the Paris Club, had no new arrears to the creditors, had met the targets of its IMF standby arrangement, and was seeking the same terms as it had received before.

Regardless of the duration of a negotiation, there is a rhythm that seldom varies from case to case. The delegations assemble in a conference room in the International Conference Center on the Avenue Kléber. They sit behind tables set in a rectangular pattern. The Chairman is at one end, with the French delegation on his right (because it is providing secretariat support) and the observers from the international organizations on his left. The debtor-country delegation occupies the end opposite the Chairman, and the creditor delegations are arrayed along the sides in alphabetical order.

Although all the negotiations from 1978 to 1984 were chaired by France, it is possible to have another country host and chair the negotiations. For example, the 1970 debt-relief negotiations with Ghana were held in London and were chaired by the British. Generically, this was still a Paris Club negotiation. On a couple of occasions during this period there were proposals to try an alternative location or chairman, but none was given serious consideration.

In a typical case, the Chairman begins the negotiations by inviting the debtor country to explain its request for relief. The debtor country is usually represented by its finance minister, but prime ministers from Jamaica in July 1984 and July 1985 and Argentina in January 1985 led their delegations to the Paris Club.

Next, the observers from international organizations are invited to make comments, starting with the IMF and followed by the World Bank, the regional development bank concerned, and UNCTAD. Finally, the creditors are given an opportunity to pose questions to the debtor-country delegation and to the observers. Most creditor delegations are led by a finance-ministry official at the level of an office director.

These preliminaries generally fill a morning session. After lunch, the creditors caucus without the debtor. They normally invite the IMF representative to attend their caucus, since the Fund sends a staff member who is intimately acquainted with the standby arrangement on which the rescheduling negotiations are based.

Discussions in the creditor caucus are sometimes more difficult and protracted than discussions with the debtor. The Chairman may open the caucus by inviting general comments, but he will be anxious to begin a preliminary "tour de table" on the main variables of a rescheduling package. As soon as possible, an initial offer is assembled consisting of the hardest position on each variable desired by any creditor, and the Chairman communicates this offer informally to the debtor-country delegation.

Since the initial offer is normally less favorable to the debtor than the terms requested, it is seldom accepted. Consequently, the caucus resumes with a report by the Chairman on the debtor's reaction. At this point, the patterns of negotiations begin to diverge. In some cases, the creditors easily agree on a second offer that is accepted. In others, the creditors will work well into the night to iron out their differences. Or the negotiations may adjourn for the day to allow both creditor and debtor delegations to seek new instructions from their capitals.

By lunchtime of the second day, it is usually possible to reach agreement on a package of terms. During the lunch break, the secretariat prepares a draft of the "Agreed Minute" containing the terms negotiated. The draft is examined after lunch, there may be some haggling on small points, and then final copies are produced in English and French, both versions being equally valid.

Rescheduling Terms

The biggest mysteries of the Paris Club process are hidden in the jargon associated with the terms of an Agreed Minute. Brief descriptions of the major terms are provided below. The specifics, however, require one observation by way of background. In some debt-relief agreements with commercial banks, the entire stock of outstanding debt on a specified date has been rescheduled or restructured.[4] Never in a Paris Club agreement. Instead, payments of principal and interest falling due in a specified time period are "consolidated" and rescheduled, and these come to represent a new layer of future payment obligations, on top of the layer already existing at the time of the negotiations. (There will soon be a third layer arising from credits signed after the conclusion of the Paris Club agreement.) The basic reason why official creditors do not reschedule the stock of debt is that it usually includes some foreign-aid credits with payments due forty to fifty years in the future. By contrast, the stock of bank debt being rescheduled rarely includes maturities more than ten years in the future.

Eligible credits. Generally, medium-term (more than one-year original maturity) credits extended by official agencies or guaranteed by them, to both public-sector and private-sector borrowers in the debtor country, are rescheduled under Paris Club agreements. Short-term credits are excluded to minimize the disruption of trade financing and to avoid administrative complications. Payments due under previous Paris Club agreements are also generally excluded.

Contract cutoff date. Payments due under credits signed after the specified cutoff date are not rescheduled. The cutoff date is usually six to twelve months before the date the rescheduling agreement is signed, but creditors have accepted cutoff dates as late as the last day before the consolidation pe-

[4] It may be useful to define precisely some of the terms used in connection with debt negotiations. "Debt reorganization" and "debt renegotiation" are virtually synonymous and are the broadest terms; they describe any change in the payments arrangements associated with an existing stock of debt, mutually agreed upon by the debtor and creditor. "Debt relief" is any deferral of arrears or of scheduled payments, or any interest-rate concession, granted by a creditor. "Restructuring" is a form of debt reorganization that modifies the stream of amortization payments relating to the whole stock of debt, normally to extend the period of repayment. "Rescheduling" is a narrower form of debt reorganization in which a limited set of payments of principal and/or interest falling due in a specific interval are deferred, leaving intact the schedule for the remaining payments. "Refinancing" is new borrowing primarily for the purpose of meeting payments on existing debt. "Refunding" is new borrowing undertaken primarily to retire (prepay) existing debt, usually to take advantage of better terms or obtain a more favorable maturity structure. Paris Club operations are strictly limited to rescheduling and refinancing. London Club operations usually involve rescheduling but sometimes involve restructuring. Refunding is not considered a form of debt relief, virtually never involves an official creditor, and is accomplished through new loans from individual lenders (or syndicates) rather than arrangements with a whole class of creditors.

riod. The creditors resist moving the cutoff date forward in successive rescheduling agreements with the same country.

Consolidation period. The most controversial variable in rescheduling agreements in recent years is probably the consolidation period: the interval during which payments falling due will be "consolidated" and rescheduled. The strong preference of creditors is to limit the consolidation period to one year coinciding with the debtor country's IMF standby arrangement. The equally strong preference of the debtor is a multi-year consolidation period of two to five years.

Including interest payments. Creditors would rather reschedule 100 percent of principal payments alone than 50 percent of principal and interest payments together, even if it means giving more relief measured in terms of current cash flow. Nevertheless, the creditors rescheduled both in most Paris Club agreements of the 1978-84 period. This was easier than providing more new aid to close the projected financing gap. Toward the end of the period, concern over comparable treatment vis-à-vis banks led creditors to reschedule a smaller percentage of interest payments than principal payments in five cases in 1983 and 1984.

Percent of payments consolidated. The deepest mystery of the Paris Club is the distinction between "consolidated" and "nonconsolidated" debt. The concept is simple enough. If a portion, 10 percent for example, of each payment falling due during the consolidation period must be paid on schedule, this portion is nonconsolidated debt. The remaining 90 percent is consolidated and rescheduled. The confusion arises because in most Paris Club agreements between 1978 and 1984 the 10 percent was also rescheduled, albeit over a shorter period of time. Furthermore, within the "nonconsolidated" portion, the debtor was required in most cases to pay a fraction on the original due dates. Ordinarily, creditors will not agree to consolidate more than 90 percent of the principal and interest payments falling due during the consolidation period.

Repayment terms. Creditors are unlikely to balk if a debtor requests a three-year grace period followed by a four-year period during which the consolidated debt is repaid in equal semiannual installments. However, in 1978-84, most grace periods were four or five years long and most repayment periods were five years or more. Still, the only agreements in which the combined grace and repayment periods were more than twelve years were those with Sudan in 1983 and 1984.

Moratorium interest. Among the major variables listed here, the only one that remained constant throughout the 1978-84 period was having the interest rate on rescheduled debt, known as "moratorium interest" in the trade, determined bilaterally. This practice is necessary because of the wide range of interest-rate structures among the creditor countries involved in the negotiations, and even among each country's creditor agencies.

De minimus creditors. To simplify implementation, minor creditors are exempted from providing relief. The limit defining a minor creditor is normally set at SDR 1 million of principal and interest payments falling due during the consolidation period. The limit has been set lower for several small debtor countries, for example, SDR 250,000 for Sierra Leone in 1984.

Boilerplate. The rescheduling terms take up about one page in the typical four-page Agreed Minute. Another page is filled with the names of all the participants and observers in the negotiation, a brief summary of the basis of the debtor's request for relief, and the creditors' response. The remainder of the text is filled with boilerplate including a nondiscrimination clause, a comparable-treatment clause, a goodwill clause (creditors agree to consider a request for further relief if warranted), and several clauses relating to exchange of information and relations with the IMF.

Implementation

Paris Club agreements are signed *ad referendum* by the heads of the delegations participating in the negotiations, who thereby agree to "recommend to their respective governments" the terms set forth in the Agreed Minute. To implement them formally, it is necessary to revise the payment obligations contained in the loan contracts concerned. Therefore, a bilateral agreement must be concluded between the debtor country and each creditor country. For some countries, including the United States, a third step is required: a rescheduling agreement must be concluded between the debtor country and each lending agency in the creditor country.

There is considerable diversity among the creditors in their approaches to implementation. Some are able to draft their bilateral agreement and present it to the debtor for signature within a month of the Paris Club negotiation. Others are notoriously slow. Some creditors send officials to the capital of the debtor country to negotiate the bilateral agreement, and the debtor country is able to obtain further concessions in these negotiations.

The most serious implementation problem in 1978-84 was the emergence of arrears on payments due under a preceding Paris Club agreement. In principle, before beginning a new round of negotiations not only must all bilateral agreements be signed but all payments due with respect to previously rescheduled debt must be paid. In practice, in a number of cases the arrears associated with this category of debt grew so large that it was not feasible for the debtor country to eliminate them by cash payment. These discouraging cases came to be known among creditors as "basket cases."

An interesting approach to these experiences emerged in 1983, motivated more by the creditors' desire to help these countries regain some semblance of creditworthiness than by their own narrow financial interests. The debtor country was asked to make monthly deposits into an account at the central bank of a creditor country beginning immediately after the conclusion of the Paris Club agreement. The sum of the deposits was calculated to be roughly equivalent to the amounts due to the creditors during the coming year under the just-concluded rescheduling agreement. As bilateral agreements were concluded, the debtor country would withdraw funds in its special account to meet obligations on the newly rescheduled debt. In this fashion, any financial incentive for the debtor to delay concluding bilateral agreements would be eliminated and there would be less likelihood that arrears on previously rescheduled debt would exist at the time of a subsequent rescheduling negotiation.

When first introduced in the Paris Club agreement with Zaire in 1983, it was envisioned that this payment mechanism would be used only in rare cases. It proved surprisingly popular, however, and was seen with some regularity in the agreements concluded during 1984. At the same time, in some cases the debtor country failed to make the agreed-upon deposits. It remains to be seen whether such offshore accounts turn out to be a fixture or a fad.

The Paris Club vs. the London Club: A Recapitulation

It may be helpful to pause here and summarize briefly the points of similarity and difference between the Paris Club and the London Club.

The two clubs are fundamentally similar in the sense that they are both *ad hoc* groups of creditors without any formal mandate or rules of procedure. The scope of the London Club is broader, however; it is able to negotiate on new credits, whereas the Paris Club will negotiate only on credits already in force.

Participation in the two clubs is different on the surface but not much different in practice. All commercial banks with exposure in the debtor country must participate in the London Club agreement with that country, but they are represented in the negotiations by a small number of the largest international banks. In Paris Club negotiations, all creditor governments may participate in principle, but the only ones that participate regularly are the major creditor governments that belong to the OECD.

The three principles of Paris Club rescheduling can be found also in London Club rescheduling, but they are applied with considerably more flexibility. For example, banks are more likely to reschedule "pre-emptively" in order to provide the debtor country with maneuvering room before it runs out of foreign exchange completely. They may also agree to reschedule without an IMF arrangement, unlike the Paris Club. The principle the banks seem most attracted to at the present time is burden sharing. In the early 1980s, the banks provided debt relief to Jamaica without any relief from official creditors. By contrast, banks effectively forced Paris Club reschedulings on Chile and Panama in 1985 even though relief may not have been justified on financial grounds. These cases seem to reflect a change in attitude on the part of the banks more than differences in the circumstances of the debtors.

There is a major difference in Paris Club and London Club documentation. In the former, a framework agreement is negotiated that will then be implemented through separate bilateral agreements with each creditor country. In the latter, a legally binding instrument is negotiated. For this reason, London Club negotiations tend to be drawn out over several months and involve significant costs charged to the debtor. By contrast, most Paris Club agreements are concluded in two days at no cost to the debtor other than travel and lodging for its own delegation.

There are also some important differences in terms. As a rule, the London Club never reschedules interest obligations, and it charges current market interest rates on rescheduled debt. This is possible because all bank lending is based on market rates so there is no inequity among banks when a single spread over a base rate (such as LIBOR) is specified for the rescheduled loans. The Paris Club, in most cases, does reschedule interest and preserves the concessionality inherent in the loans being rescheduled. This means that the average interest on the rescheduled credits of a creditor which has given predominantly concessional credits will be much lower than the average interest on the rescheduled credits of another creditor which extended exclusively nonconcessional credits. Finally, the Paris Club strongly resists consolidation periods longer than one year, while the London Club prefers agreements extending over two or three years when it is clear that several years of relief will be required.

4 The Paris Club in North-South Politics

Debt did not emerge as a major North-South issue until the Fourth United Nations Conference on Trade and Development (UNCTAD IV) held in Nairobi in 1976. During the next four years, as North-South negotiations reached a crescendo and then began to fizzle out, debt was never at the very top of the agenda of the developing-country bloc (the Group of 77, or G-77), but it was continuously among the top three or four issues.

Concern about debt was obviously precipitated by the widespread balance-of-payments problems that flared up among developing countries following the oil-price increases of 1973-74. There had been latent interest in generalized debt relief for developing countries before UNCTAD IV, largely associated with the balance-of-payments difficulties of India and Pakistan in the 1960s. At Nairobi in 1976 a new debt issue crystallized. The G-77 sought to replace the Paris Club approach to debt relief with a more formally institutionalized approach favoring their interests. The industrialized countries were adamantly opposed to such a change, but they eventually supported UNCTAD Resolution 94(IV), which called for an attempt to find a set of principles or "features" to govern debt-relief negotiations that would be acceptable to both creditors and debtors. Consequently, the UNCTAD secretariat convened a series of meetings of debt experts to work on debt-relief features. Parallel discussions on debt took place in the inconclusive Conference on International Economic Cooperation (CIEC) in 1976-77.

Shortly thereafter, at a special meeting of the UNCTAD Trade and Development Board (TDB) in Geneva in March 1978, the spotlight returned to the issue of generalized debt relief. Pressure on the industrialized countries to do something in the debt area had intensified, and they responded by accepting a two-part resolution.

Part A of TDB Resolution 165(S-IX) responded to G-77 demands for generalized debt relief. The industrialized countries committed themselves to "seek to adopt" certain measures for the benefit of a limited group of the poorer developing countries. Specifically, they were to convert outstanding aid loans to these countries to grants. This would have made their past practice consistent with their current practice of extending *new* aid to the poorest countries strictly in the form of grants. The euphemism for this procedure was "retroactive terms adjustment," or simply RTA. Several qualifications were included in the resolution to distinguish RTA from debt relief or debt forgiveness.

The industrialized countries implemented RTA in quite different ways. At one extreme, a few countries simply wrote off old debts and even extended the practice to poor countries beyond those on the United Nations' list of the least developed. Other countries provided additional amounts of fast-disbursing grant assistance to offset payments due on old loans, one year at a time. The United States never implemented RTA, and this has remained a lingering but minor issue in UNCTAD. Legislation was proposed by the Carter Administration and was passed by the Senate, but it was rejected by the House. Even though the cost of the proposed RTA was estimated to be only about $15 million per year, the opponents argued that, at the margin, scarce aid funds could better be used in other countries or for specific projects that would yield tangible results.

Part B of the TDB Resolution carried the work on debt-relief "features" one step forward. It identified four basic concepts to serve as the foundation for further negotiations. A year later, in 1979, the most intensive round of negotiations took place at UNCTAD V in Manila. The G-77 arrived with the objective of establishing an International Debt Commission, a new and permanent institution to replace both the Paris Club and the London Club. The industrialized countries were equally intent on preserving the existing *ad hoc* procedures, and no compromise was possible.

Remarkably, a compromise of sorts was reached at a TDB meeting in Geneva in October 1980. Another two-part resolution, TDB Resolution 222(XXI), was adopted. Part A did little more than reaffirm the earlier commitment by industrialized countries to grant RTA to the poorer developing countries. Part B contained the endorsement by all UNCTAD members of "Detailed Features for Future Operations Relating to the Debt Problems of Interested Developing Countries." While the language contains a number of ambiguities that the industrialized countries tried unsuccessfully to eliminate, it may be taken as a general endorsement of traditional Paris Club procedures. It can thus be regarded as testimony to the weakness of the G-77 by 1980. A more benign interpretation is that the pragmatists among the G-77 recognized that debt relief "on demand" would probably not solve debt problems but would almost certainly discourage new flows of loans and grants to developing countries, and that the pragmatists were able to persuade their bloc that the creditors were not prepared to abandon the Paris Club.

The industrialized countries made one significant concession to obtain G-77 support for the Paris Club. They accepted a continuing interest by UNCTAD in the debt-rescheduling process. This concession could come back to haunt the creditors. It can be argued, however, that this concession had already been granted in 1979, when an observer from the UNCTAD secretariat was invited for the first time to attend a Paris Club negotiation (with Togo). The earlier concession essentially undercut the G-77 in the North-South negotiations on debt. The French were especially keen to gain a G-77 endorsement of the Paris Club process and saw the presence of an UNCTAD observer as a low-cost gesture. Other, less important gestures were made by the Paris Club creditors in response to G-77 concerns in the 1978-84 period. The site of the Paris Club negotiations was moved from the offices of the French Treasury to the International Conference Center. In addition, the French secretariat tried to make the Paris Club more friendly by means of more frequent and more diplomatic contacts with potential debt-relief applicants.

After 1980, debt faded temporarily from the scene as a North-South issue. When it reemerged in 1983-84, the venue was not UNCTAD but various Latin American groups: the Organization of American States, the Economic Commission for Latin America and the Caribbean, Sistema Económico Latinoamericano, and most notably the informal Cartagena group. It is too early to say how far these efforts will go, but it is fascinating to see how the various regional groups within the G-77 have divided on the debt issue. The Asian countries have adopted the position that was originally expressed most forcefully by the Latin American group in the 1976-80 North-South negotiations. Debt relief is a concern limited to "interested" developing countries, and the Asian countries are not interested. The Latin Americans are now preoccupied with the carrying costs of their rescheduling agreements with commercial banks. The Africans have replaced Pakistan and India as the chief advocates of debt forgiveness. By the fall of 1985, the pressures on creditors to respond to the evolving economic and political situation in debtor countries led to proposals by the United States to modify the three-year-old strategy for addressing the debt problems of these countries. These modifications are discussed briefly in section 6.

5 Challenges to the Paris Club

Two challenges face the Paris Club today. The first is that a number of debtor countries appear to be caught in a form of "debt trap" that brings them back to the Paris Club year after year. The second is that a few debtor countries have tried to impose unilateral debt-rescheduling arrangements upon official creditor agencies that have made loans to their private-sector borrowers.

Serial Rescheduling

In an earlier section of this essay, conditionality was cited as the major determinant of success or failure for a Paris Club rescheduling. There is, of course, a simple-minded standard of success. If a country comes to the Paris Club once and never needs debt relief again, this is clearly a success. The Paris Club rescheduling may be only one of a number of elements that contribute to reestablishing the country's creditworthiness, but it is bound to be an important and necessary element.

Now look at the record. Of the 29 countries that received debt relief in the Paris Club from 1978 to 1984, only 2 (Gabon and Mexico) came once and are not expected to return.[5] By the simple-minded standard, then, 27 of these 29 cases were failures. But this standard is unfair, for two reasons.

First, the practice of the Paris Club creditors is to grant relief only in respect of payments falling due during a single twelve-month period. Even when a longer period of relief appears necessary and justifiable from the outset, the creditors insist that a follow-up arrangement be negotiated later. Not only is it difficult to forecast balance-of-payments developments more than a year ahead, but the Paris Club creditors want to strengthen the incentives for effective implementation of its adjustment program by keeping the debtor country on a "short leash." Among the countries that came to the Paris Club between 1978 and 1984, three came back during this period but appeared to

[5] The Appendix provides a complete listing of the Paris Club agreements concluded in this period, showing the amounts involved and the general terms.

have overcome their debt problems by the end of the period: Malawi, Romania, and Turkey. These should also be considered successes.

The second reason for seeking a better measure of success is that every rescheduling agreement is premised on a number of assumptions and estimates, and these can be wrong. In the 1978-84 period, serious mistakes were made in estimating (a) the amount of debt owed by the debtor country and the associated debt-service obligations, and (b) the prices of the debtors' major exports, for example, copper.

In the rush to prevent debt problems from damaging an economy, debt-relief arrangements are occasionally negotiated before a full inventory of external debt has been completed. In some cases, new governments have no record of certain obligations; in other cases, the records have been scattered among different ministries and are inaccurate. Follow-up rescheduling operations that arise from problems of this sort cannot be taken as proof that the Paris Club process has failed. The same must be said about changing export (or import) prices; the changes are generally beyond the control of the debtor country or its creditors. However, no case in the 1978-84 period clearly belongs to this additional class of cases that cannot be considered failures.

Is it necessary to conclude, then, that the remaining twenty-four countries represent Paris Club failures? The global economic environment was very difficult for debtor countries during the 1978-84 period. It is possible that the environment in the second half of the 1980s will quickly become more favorable. If so, many of these countries will not need further debt relief and in retrospect will be considered Paris Club successes.

Creditor-country rescheduling experts are strongly inclined to point the finger at poor economic policies in the debtor countries as the main reason for the small number of "successes" in the 1978-84 period. Specifically, in at least half of the twenty-four remaining cases, the debt relief granted by the Paris Club creditors went to waste because debtor countries failed to follow through with policy reforms they had promised to undertake in conjunction with their IMF standby arrangements. When exchange rates remained overvalued, government budget deficits increased as a percentage of GNP, and domestic agricultural production was discouraged by price controls, obviously countries in the midst of debt crises were not going to strengthen their balance-of-payments positions and end up with enough foreign exchange to meet the claims of their external creditors. With better policy performance in the initial stages of their debt crises, countries like the Ivory Coast, Senegal, Costa Rica, and Ecuador might well have "graduated" from the Paris Club by the end of 1984. From the same point of view, even with the most favorable imaginable global economic situation, debtor countries with inappropriate policies would not have recovered their creditworthiness.

The Paris Club negotiators from the major creditor countries are, however, especially concerned about a group of countries that seem caught in a pattern of "serial rescheduling." From the beginning of 1978 through October 1985, Togo made five trips to the Paris Club, and Liberia, Madagascar, Senegal, Sudan, and Zaire each made four trips. Zaire holds the record for the longest period of continuous debt relief—almost ten years—including three separate Paris Club agreements negotiated in 1976 and 1977. Outside of sub-Sahara Africa, Cuba made its third trip in mid-1985, and the debt situations of Morocco, Jamaica, and Peru seem far from being stabilized. Is it possible that the Paris Club approach has contributed to these prolonged problems?

To open the debate, it is worth noting that a mathematical imperative operates in a debt crisis. Debt-service obligations are not reduced when they are rescheduled: they are increased, because interest is charged on the debt being rescheduled. Consequently, there is a snowball effect when a country returns in successive years for more debt relief and each new agreement covers principal and interest payments due on previously rescheduled debt. (Since most Paris Club reschedulings have an element of concessionality, there is no increase in the present value of the obligations when discounted at market rates of interest.)

Sudan offers the most dramatic illustration of snowballing debt. The debt-relief terms granted to Sudan by the Paris Club creditors in 1979 were quite ordinary. In 1982, Sudan came back for an additional eighteen months of relief. To provide sufficient relief on that occasion, the creditors rescheduled loans extended after the initial rescheduling (contrary to normal practice), increased to 90 the percentage of payments rescheduled, and made the grace period five years long. When Sudan came back for more relief in 1983, recent loans were again included, previously rescheduled debt was included, the percentage rescheduled was raised to 100, and a sixteen-year repayment period was granted, including six years of grace. The creditors also took the unprecedented step of capitalizing into the rescheduled debt one-half of the interest due in 1983 on the amount previously rescheduled. By this time, payments on rescheduled debt were considerably larger than the unrescheduled payments falling due during the consolidation period.

In the rescheduling for 1983, roughly $540 million in arrears and payments falling due in 1983 was deferred, while the interest payable on the deferred amount during 1983 was reduced to only $20 million. Essentially the same terms were extended for 1984. Nevertheless, at the beginning of 1985, Sudan appeared to have less hard currency available for debt service than it had in 1984. To top it off, Sudan's arrears to the IMF exceeded $100 million, and the IMF was unwilling to conclude a new standby arrangement until these were eliminated.

In 1970, faced with a somewhat similar situation in Indonesia, the Paris Club creditors had agreed to a remarkable package of terms designed by a

German banker, Dr. Hermann Abs, who had been recruited by the creditors to find an innovative solution to Indonesia's debt problem. Indonesia was allowed to work off its rescheduled debt over thirty years, and no interest was charged on the unpaid balance. This eliminated the snowball effect, although the oil-price increases that began in 1973-74 and good economic management probably had more to do with the restoration of Indonesia's creditworthiness.

A French banker was recruited to offer suggestions for the Sudan rescheduling of 1983, but he met with much less success, for three reasons. First and most important, Sudan was unable to implement policy reforms that would justify an exceptional effort by the creditors of the sort made for Indonesia. On the contrary, measures such as the introduction of Islamic law strengthened antigovernment forces in southern Sudan, and caused work to be stopped on an oil pipeline that the creditors were hoping would be Sudan's financial salvation. These measures contributed to the coup d'état in 1985. Second, commercial banks were not significant creditors of Indonesia, but they were large creditors of Sudan. The banks could not contemplate Indonesia-style terms, and the official creditors were bound by the principle of comparable treatment to offer terms roughly similar to those offered by the banks. Third, there were only two Paris Club negotiations in 1970, when Indonesia came to the Paris Club. By contrast, more than twenty other countries were lined up at the door of the Paris Club when the time came to consider Sudan's case. If the creditors offered exceptionally generous terms to Sudan, it would be politically awkward for them to deny similar terms to many of these applicants, even if they did not need such treatment.

It is tempting to conclude from the Sudanese case that the Paris Club approach made Sudan's debt problem worse, but what alternative would have been better? Official creditors can be extremely flexible in setting Paris Club terms when the circumstances justify it. Attempts to be more generous tend to backfire, because the creditors simply make offsetting reductions in new financing or the debtors use the extra maneuvering room to delay inevitable policy reforms. If there is a hidden flaw in the creditors' treatment of Sudan, it is that they continued to extend new loans to Sudan after the first rescheduling. (The commercial banks, by contrast, stopped lending cold.) Most of these new loans were on highly concessional terms, but a significant number were on commercial or near-commercial terms, including some for purchases of military hardware that contributed nothing to the ability of the Sudanese economy to service foreign debt.

If these loans had been grants instead, Sudan's debt problem in 1985 would have been considerably more manageable. From a theoretical perspective, there are strong arguments for providing external financing strictly in the form of grants when a country seeking debt relief appears to have a chronic balance-of-payments problem. In practice, however, most governments have to operate with programs that are limited by law to the use of loans. In the case of the United States, for example, the Export-Import Bank is unable to provide grant financing. In addition, until fiscal year 1985 very little grant financing was available for U.S. military sales. Political realities occasionally overwhelm financial prudence and lock creditors and debtors together in a vicious cycle.

Before concluding that political constraints are a critical problem for creditors, however, it is instructive to look at Turkey, the biggest success among the Paris Club's clients in the 1978-84 period. In 1979, Turkey's debt problem was viewed by creditors as comparable in severity to those of Sudan and Zaire. They were impressed, however, by the policy reforms undertaken by a new Turkish government at the beginning of 1980, and they bent their rules to offer Turkey a three-year debt-relief package that included relief on previously rescheduled debt during the first year. In addition, they provided a $1.2 billion package of new fast-disbursing loan and grant aid.

The recovery of the Turkish economy exceeded the expectations of the most sanguine observers, and Turkey did not seek further relief at the end of its 1980-83 consolidation period. Its debt burden at the beginning of 1985 appeared large but manageable. While Turkey benefited unexpectedly from the Iran-Iraq conflict, declining oil prices, and other exogenous factors, Turkey's success is clearly and primarily attributable to its policy reforms and the vigor with which they were implemented. Debt relief received in the Paris and London Clubs was an essential but strictly secondary factor.

The case of Zaire, by contrast, illustrates the cyclical element in the problem of serial rescheduling that looms so large at this juncture. Zaire is the Paris Club's steadiest client. To the surprise of most creditors, Zaire made all the monthly payments into its offshore account required in 1984, and it entered 1985 with a stronger than anticipated balance-of-payments position. Persistence in implementing policy reforms, after years of saying one thing and doing another, accounted for much of this success, but rising copper prices were probably more important in financial terms. If the current trend continues, foreign donors, creditors, and investors will presumably provide increased financing to Zaire, and capital flight will be reversed. Think of the mood of optimism that will exist and the financial benefits it will bring when Zaire announces that further debt relief is not needed!

A more complex factor in serial rescheduling is the role of the IMF. Paris Club creditors have mixed feelings about extensions of Fund credit to countries with chronic debt problems. Obviously, financing provided by the IMF reduces the amount of debt relief or new aid that official creditors have to provide. But IMF financing is relatively "hard" and debt service to the IMF is exempt by tradition from rescheduling. Consequently, continuing deterioration in a debtor's balance-of-payments situation after an initial rescheduling has the effect of shifting to the IMF a progressively larger share of the debtor's foreign-exchange receipts. If payments difficulties continue, arrears to the IMF may start building up quickly. This happened in Sudan and several other countries. These arrears to the Fund will have to be paid off before these countries can conclude new standby arrangements, which will then allow them to get more debt relief. Friendly donor governments are the most likely source of foreign exchange to eliminate arrears to the IMF.

One way to avoid this kind of trap is for the IMF to negotiate a standby arrangement with the debtor country that involves only a token amount of IMF financing and therefore modest repayment obligations to the Fund. The drawback to this solution is that debtor governments generally are unwilling to undertake reforms unless the IMF provides them with a large amount of financing. Here is another example of political realities interfering with financial rationality.

In October 1985, the U.S. government proposed a new approach that was clearly designed with an eye on low-income countries caught in a pattern of serial rescheduling. The approach involved the use of repayments to the IMF Trust Fund, as well as other multilateral and bilateral resources, to support comprehensive economic reform programs in the poorest developing countries (see section 6).

Unilateral Rescheduling

After the problem of serial rescheduling, the most difficult problem facing Paris Club creditors at the end of 1984 was the attempt by several debtor countries to introduce schemes to reschedule the obligations of their private-sector borrowers to official agencies without negotiations in the Paris Club—that is, unilaterally. The problem is so complicated that it can best be described by walking through a specific case. The Mexican case is an especially good example because it is the only case in Paris Club history in which the rescheduled debt was exclusively private-sector debt.

After reaching broad agreement with commercial banks in 1982 on rescheduling their credits to Mexican borrowers, both public and private, the government of Mexico concluded that it would not need to reschedule official and officially guaranteed credits if official export-credit agencies did not withdraw cover for new business. But Mexico made a major miscalculation that became apparent only in the final stages of its negotiations with the IMF and the London Club. The government had assumed that all private-sector debts could be rescheduled in the same fashion, whether the creditor was private or official. A complicated scheme had been established, based on a trust fund known as FICORCA, to reschedule private-sector obligations. The Mexican government sold forward foreign exchange through FICORCA to private-sector borrowers so that they would be able to meet their future debt-service obligations, and it offered more favorable peso/dollar exchange rates to those borrowers who were able to obtain longer repayment terms from their foreign creditors. Since many of these borrowers were illiquid at the current exchange rate, moreover, the government offered them local-currency loans to purchase forward exchange through FICORCA.

The scheme ran afoul of the creditor governments. They had agreed to continue providing export credits to Mexico on the understanding that their credits would not be rescheduled—including some $2-$3 billion of credits to private-sector borrowers. They were not at all pleased to learn that Mexico intended to include these credits in its FICORCA scheme, which they viewed as a unilateral arrangement. They insisted that Mexico negotiate a proper rescheduling arrangement for these credits in the Paris Club.

The negotiations were protracted and unusually contentious. The Mexican government would not agree to take the credits concerned out of the FICORCA scheme and reschedule them in the normal fashion. For their part, the creditors were bullheaded in trying to impose on the Mexican government a substantial responsibility for the "commercial risk" associated with these credits.

The concept of commercial risk is central to the problem of rescheduling private-sector debt. When a foreign creditor makes a loan to a private-sector borrower without a guarantee from the borrowing country's government, the creditor bears all the commercial risk. If the borrower does not have enough local currency to buy foreign exchange from the authorities at the rate specified for foreign debt-service payments, its creditors can seek a bankruptcy judgment against it in the local courts and obtain whatever satisfaction local laws allow. But the creditors have no claim on the government of the borrower's country. By contrast, if the borrower deposits the requisite amount of local currency with the authorities, but the government does not have enough foreign exchange to meet all of its debtors' obligations, creditors do have a claim on the government.

In practice, however, it is seldom so neat and tidy. For example, Mexican private-sector borrowers were able to buy a dollar for 26 pesos at the beginning of February 1982, but they had to pay 49 pesos in August and 95 pesos by the end of December. At 26 pesos to the dollar, most borrowers had no difficulty meeting their obligations to foreign creditors; at 95 to the dollar, many borrowers were insolvent.

The Mexican government could have turned its back on these borrowers and left their foreign creditors with no recourse but to initiate bankruptcy proceedings in the Mexican courts. Realizing that this "shock treatment" would damage its economy as well as alienate foreign creditors, the government devised the FICORCA scheme to spread out the shock over six to eight years. But then it tried to have its cake and eat it too. The Mexican government argued in the Paris Club that if a borrower defaulted *for any reason* on the loan it had taken from the Mexican government in order to buy forward foreign exchange, the Mexican government would have no obligation to make the corresponding foreign-exchange payments to the borrower's foreign creditors. In the eyes of the Paris Club creditors, this position smacked of bad faith because it looked like a cheap way to save foreign exchange. The Mexican government would only have had to lose a few checks or suggest that a borrower stop repaying its peso loans from the government.

In the Paris Club negotiations of June 1983, a device was found to paper over the differences and permit an agreement to be signed. But it proved to be unworkable when examined closely, and another six months of tough negotiating were required before the first bilateral agreement could be signed. The experience soured the Mexicans on the Paris Club to such an extent that they decided not to seek the second year of relief that the creditors were prepared in principle to offer. Needless to say, the creditors were delighted by the Mexican decision.

Before the Mexican case was resolved, the Paris Club creditors found themselves facing similar problems with Nigeria and Venezuela. When these countries began to experience balance-of-payments difficulties, their governments stopped making foreign exchange available for debt-service payments by private-sector borrowers but continued to meet their public-sector obligations. The governments never thought to distinguish between obligations to official creditors and those to private creditors, and they proceeded to establish facilities that would assist private-sector borrowers to defer their payments to foreign creditors.

The schemes were variations on the Mexican approach. The government of Nigeria issued bonds redeemable in the future in foreign currency against the deposit of local currency. The government of Venezuela simply issued a regulation to the effect that private-sector borrowers able to get their foreign creditors to reschedule overdue principal payments over seven years would be eligible to buy foreign exchange for their obligations to these creditors at a preferential rate. These are only two of many possible variations on the basic scheme of forcing borrowers to reschedule their foreign debt through special exchange-rate or deferred-payment arrangements. The rates of conversion can be varied according to the purpose of the borrowing (a less favorable rate for luxury goods than for capital equipment) or the length of time the hard-currency payment will be deferred. Interest payments can be converted at one rate and principal payments at another. The bonds issued can earn interest at floating-market rates or less attractive ones. Obviously, schemes of this kind can be administrative nightmares—especially when the government insists on verifying each application and rejects some for minor administrative violations.

In the Nigerian and Venezuelan cases, the Paris Club creditors slowly became aware that arrears were accumulating, and their export-credit agencies made inquiries to determine the cause. When they learned the arrears were not due to commercial failure, they made representations to the governments. Eventually, the problems surfaced in one of the informal "tours d'horizon" within the creditor caucus that is held before, during, or after most Paris Club negotiating sessions.

Following a well-established procedure, the creditors agreed that the Chairman of the Paris Club should send messages to Nigeria and Venezuela conveying the concerns of the creditors and urging the governments to make foreign exchange available for debt service as quickly as possible. These messages were repeated or elaborated upon when they met with silence or an unsatisfactory response. But they did not have the desired effect of eliminating the arrears.

The Nigerian and Venezuelan cases differed from the Mexican in two other respects. First, neither country intended to conclude a standby arrangement with the IMF. This placed the creditors in an awkward situation. If they negotiated rescheduling agreements, they would have to ignore the principle of conditionality. If, instead, they simply accepted the unilaterally imposed deferment schemes, they might be encouraging unilateral rescheduling by other debtor countries. Second, neither country met all the criteria for being in a position of imminent default. Venezuela, in particular, had accumulated foreign-exchange reserves substantially larger than its arrears.

These cases warrant an extended discussion because they reflect an aspect of the rescheduling process that is likely to become more important in the years ahead. At present, the majority of Paris Club clients are countries with weak private sectors that do relatively little foreign borrowing. If current trends continue, however, private-sector debt will grow relative to public-sector debt, and future Paris Club clients are more likely to have a substantial amount of private-sector debt.

The worst solution to the problem would be to insist that all official and officially guaranteed credits to private-sector borrowers be guaranteed by the government of the borrowing country. This would tend to misallocate investment and would relieve official creditor agencies of the commercial risk that they properly should bear. It might be better for the export-credit agencies, which account for the vast bulk of official credits to private-sector borrowers, to negotiate umbrella agreements with the governments of countries in which private-sector borrowing is becoming large. These agreements might include commitments by the debtor governments to differentiate between official and private credits if they find themselves unable to provide foreign exchange to meet all the external obligations of the private sector. In return, the export-credit agencies might agree to accept deferred-payment bonds with certain characteristics (maximum term of four years, no discrimination among creditors, exchange rates no worse than for public-sector borrowers, no differentiation by purpose of the credit) in lieu of a formal multilateral rescheduling.

6 The Five-Point Debt Strategy

The debt problems of developing countries did not become a matter of global concern until August 1982, when Mexico announced that it would no longer be able to pay its external creditors on schedule. But the Mexican announcement was not a complete surprise. The Zaire reschedulings of 1976-77 were a first warning that commercial-bank debt was vulnerable. The Turkish reschedulings of 1978-80 were massive in relation to all previous experience and involved virtually all the complexities of later cases. The Polish rescheduling in 1981 taught all creditors to re-examine the assumptions that underlay their assessments of the risk associated with sovereign lending.

Anxieties peaked in late 1982 and early 1983, however, when Mexico's difficulties spilled over to Brazil and the dispute over the Falkland Islands interrupted loan payments from Argentina. At this point, three of the world's five largest debtors were on the critical list, and their creditors around the world were having palpitations. There were intense political pressures for governments to act in a visible manner. Problems of this magnitude could not be left in the hands of the Paris Club technicians!

A multitude of schemes and approaches were proposed from every quarter, but the strategy selected in the end was one that was thoroughly grounded in a generation of Paris Club experience. The strategy was first articulated by the U.S. government at the end of 1982 and was subsequently endorsed during 1983 in major economic forums, including the Williamsburg Summit, the Ministerial meeting of the OECD, and the IMF Interim Committee. It consisted of five elements:

- Effective economic-adjustment measures by the debtor countries in difficulty
- A central role for the IMF in supporting these adjustment measures
- Additional commercial-bank lending to countries pursuing sound adjustment programs
- "Bridge financing" from creditor-country governments and central banks in selected cases
- Stable, noninflationary growth in the industrial countries without any new barriers to imports from debtor countries.

The first three elements echoed the Paris Club principles of conditionality and burden sharing. The last two were in no way inconsistent with Paris Club practices. Consequently, the experts who represented creditor countries in the Paris Club took comfort in the strategy and proceeded with their business without a break in stride.

After a year of applying the strategy, however, critics from the debtor-country perspective complained that the strategy was nothing more than the classic case-by-case approach. On the other side, commercial banks complained that governments were not doing enough to solve debt problems. Specifically, while banks were prepared to conclude multi-year rescheduling agreements, governments were reluctant.

Neither criticism was well founded. Considerable adaptibility was demonstrated in the reschedulings with Sudan and Mexico in 1983. More could have been demonstrated had circumstances warranted it. In addition, while new official financing was excluded for reasons of principle from Paris Club arrangements, official export-credit agencies were stepping in to provide financing to those countries of greatest concern to the banks. Furthermore, official creditors were rescheduling interest payments, which was financially equivalent to the "new lending" provided by banks. And the banks had a narrow self-interested reason for preferring multi-year arrangements—their negotiations are quite costly and time-consuming.

Eventually, political pressures prevailed over expert opinion and the debt strategy was amended in 1984, at the London Summit, to include the multi-year rescheduling option. But the lessons learned in the extended reschedulings of 1978-81 were not forgotten: the new option was heavily qualified. Multi-year rescheduling agreements would be offered only to countries that had demonstrated success in their adjustment efforts and were not expected to need further debt relief at the end of the multi-year rescheduling period. In short, multi-year agreements would not be offered to countries that were locked in a pattern of serial rescheduling.

Even with a mandate from the seven Summit powers, it was not until the rescheduling arrangement with Ecuador, on the eve of the 1985 Summit in Bonn, that the Paris Club negotiated a multi-year agreement. In the process, a new form of Paris Club conditionality was developed. Commercial banks, in their negotiations with Mexico in 1984, had agreed to grant debt relief on a multi-year basis without conditioning the relief on the usual borrowing arrangement with the IMF. With strong support from governments in the major creditor countries, the IMF developed the concept of "enhanced surveillance" to provide some assurance to the banks that Mexico would continue to follow sound policies. In 1985, the banks concluded similar debt-relief agreements with Venezuela and Ecuador. In designing their multi-year rescheduling agreement with Ecuador, the Paris Club creditors adopted a form of enhanced surveillance. Relief in the first two years was linked to an IMF standby arrangement in the usual manner. The third year of relief permitted, at the discretion of creditors, enhanced surveillance by the IMF as an alternative to a follow-on standby. The enhanced surveillance, however, was a more specific and quantitative form than that used by the commercial banks in their arrangements with Mexico, Venezuela, and Ecuador. In all likelihood, this so-called "enhanced surveillance" by the IMF will be a more significant innovation than the multi-year feature itself.

Later in 1985, a more dramatic elaboration of the debt strategy was unveiled by U.S. Treasury Secretary James Baker at the annual meetings of the IMF and World Bank in Seoul, Korea. He proposed a "Program for Sustained Growth" for fifteen major debtor countries that have had recourse to debt relief or involuntary lending arrangements with their commercial-bank creditors. The program included three elements: (a) adoption by these debtor countries of comprehensive growth-oriented structural-reform programs; (b) net new commercial-bank lending amounting to $20 billion over the period 1986-88; and (c) expanded policy-linked lending by multilateral development banks amounting to $27 billion over the same period.

For low-income countries with protracted debt problems, especially those in Africa, Secretary Baker proposed a more intensive form of collaboration between the IMF and the World Bank. Well-conceived adjustment programs would be supported by means of highly concessional loans funded by the $2.7 billion of reflows to the IMF Trust Fund anticipated during the 1986-91 period and an equivalent amount of World Bank resources.

The motives behind these improvements in the five-point debt strategy should not be difficult to discern. The initiative on behalf of the major debtors reflected concern that debtor-country adjustment efforts to date had focused primarily on ameliorating external financial constraints without adequately addressing the fundamental structural reforms needed to achieve sustained economic growth. It also reflected concern that well-conceived reforms would not lead to sufficient growth unless commercial banks provided additional net financing. The initiative on behalf of low-income debtors was designed to deal with their problems in a comprehensive manner that would result in consistent policy advice from the IMF and the World Bank and in additional external financing. Such an approach was considered necessary to prevent the problem of serial rescheduling (compounded by arrears to the IMF) from spreading.

Both efforts were designed to take the initiative at a time when the major creditor countries saw no real likelihood that the debt problems of developing countries would be eliminated through rapid economic growth in those countries, better access for their exports, or higher levels of official financing or direct investment. Without abandoning the case-by-case approach to debt problems or recognition of the importance of debtor-country adjustment, the time had come to give greater emphasis to developing-country growth.

The proposals were received positively by the financial community in general, although bankers and debtor countries predictably expressed various reservations about how the proposals woud be implemented. Nevertheless, the odds are high that both proposals will be implemented, because the alternatives are distinctly less attractive and feasible.

Further "elaborations" on the debt strategy will undoubtedly be adopted if debt-servicing pressures on the debtor countries intensify. Better yet, if the pressures lessen, the debt strategy will fade into oblivion. By contrast, the Paris Club is here to stay. Even with the best imaginable global economic environment, an occasional country will have a streak of bad luck or bad management and require debt relief. Rescheduling in the Paris Club (and the London Club) is an approach to these problems that fits comfortably into the existing international financial and monetary systems. It will endure for as long as those systems themselves.

* * * * *

In conclusion, the Paris Club has played a major role in managing the debt problems that shook the international financial system in the early 1980s. I have devoted more words in this essay to the weaknesses of the Paris Club than to its strengths, but only because the weaknesses are more interesting.

From a creditor country's perspective, the strengths unquestionably overwhelm the weaknesses. If the Paris Club had not existed earlier, it would have been invented in the 1980s, probably in very much the same form. Having established a respectable track record, it provided a model for commercial banks when they had to develop standard rescheduling procedures. The Paris Club also provided a set of principles and fresh experience that were reassuring in the darkest days of 1982 and 1983 and that became the basis of the strategy adopted for shepherding creditors and debtors through their difficulties. The proven adaptability of the Paris Club makes it likely that current problems, such as unilateral rescheduling, will be solved in due course.

From a debtor country's perspective, the record may be more ambiguous. Time will tell, but I suspect that the Paris Club will survive for many years to come and that more of today's debtors, such as Mexico and Brazil, will find themselves on the creditor side of the table. Furthermore, sound policies and a favorable global environment may reduce the problem of serial rescheduling to a couple of cases a year. Alternatively, if debtors find it progressively harder to escape the snowball effect of repeated reschedulings, the Paris Club should be able to find solutions that minimize the adverse consequences for more creditworthy countries but also offer hope for countries caught in the trap.

References

E. Brau, R. C. Williams, *et al.*, *Recent Multilateral Debt Restructurings with Official and Bank Creditors*, Occasional Paper No. 25, Washington, International Monetary Fund, 1983.

E. Brau and C. Puckahtikom, *Export Credit Cover Policies and Payments Difficulties*, Occasional Paper No. 37, Washington, International Monetary Fund, 1985.

Rieffel, Alexis, "The Paris Club, 1978-83," *Columbia Journal of Transnational Law*, 23 (No. 1, 1984).

APPENDIX
Paris Club Agreements, 1978-1984

Country	Agreed Minute Signed	Consolidation Period	Percent Consolidated	Repayment of Consolidated Debt[a] First	Repayment of Consolidated Debt[a] Last	Amount of Rescheduled Debt[b] (millions of $) Paris Club	Amount of Rescheduled Debt[b] (millions of $) U.S.	Remarks[c]
Gabon	06/20/78	[d]	80	1979	1987	$ 60	$ 0	ar
Turkey	05/20/78	05/21/78-06/30/79	80	06/30/81	12/31/85	1,200	190	ar,st,nc
Peru	11/03/78	01/01/79-12/31/79	90	01/01/82	06/30/86	580	105	p
	and	01/01/80-12/31/80	90	01/01/83	06/30/86			p,imf
Togo	06/15/79	04/06/79-03/31/80	80	12/31/82	06/30/88	220	2	ar
	and	04/01/80-12/31/80	80	12/31/83	06/30/89			imf
Turkey	07/25/79	07/01/79-06/30/80	85	07/01/83	01/01/88	850	165	nc
Sudan	11/13/79	10/01/79-06/30/80	85	06/30/83	12/31/89	480	20	ar
	and	07/01/80-06/30/81	85	06/30/84	12/31/90			imf
Zaire	12/11/79	07/01/79-06/30/80	90	06/30/84	12/31/89	1,200	450	cc,ar,nc st
	and	07/01/80-12/31/80	90	06/30/84	12/31/89			imf
Sierra Leone	02/08/80	07/01/79-10/31/80	90	12/31/84	06/30/90	20	0	ar,nc
	and	11/01/80-12/31/81	90	12/31/85	06/30/91			nc,imf
Turkey	07/23/80	07/01/80-06/30/81	90	01/01/86	07/01/90	3,000	720	cc,ar,nc st,pr
	and	07/01/81-06/30/82	90	01/01/87	07/01/91			nc,imf
	and	07/01/82-06/30/83	90	01/01/88	07/01/92			nc,imf

Country	Agreed Minute Signed	Consolidation Period	Percent Consolidated	Repayment of Consolidated Debt[a] First	Repayment of Consolidated Debt[a] Last	Amount of Rescheduled Debt[b] (millions of $) Paris Club	Amount of Rescheduled Debt[b] (millions of $) U.S.	Remarks[c]
Liberia	12/19/80	07/01/80-12/31/81	90	03/31/85	09/30/89	$ 20	$ 10	nc
Togo	02/20/81	01/01/81-12/31/81	85	12/31/85	06/30/90	230	2	cc,nc
	and	01/01/82-12/31/82	85	12/31/86	06/30/91			imf
Poland	04/27/81	05/01/81-12/31/81	90	01/01/86	07/01/89	2,900	380	ar
Madagascar	04/30/81	01/01/81-06/30/82	85	03/31/86	09/30/90	300	0	ar,st,nc
Cent. Afr. Republic	06/12/81	01/01/81-12/31/81	85	12/31/85	06/30/90	50	10	ar
Zaire	07/09/81	01/01/81-12/31/81	90	12/31/85	06/30/91	610	145	nc
	and	01/01/82-12/31/82	90	12/31/86	06/30/92			nc,imf
Senegal	10/13/81	07/01/81-06/30/82	85	06/30/86	12/31/90	70	5	nc
Uganda	11/18/81	07/01/81-06/30/82	90	12/31/86	06/30/91	50	5	ar,nc
Liberia	12/16/81	01/01/82-09/30/82	90	11/15/86	05/15/91	25	10	nc
	and	10/01/82-06/30/83	90	08/15/87	02/15/92			nc,imf
Sudan	03/18/82	07/01/81-12/31/82	90	07/01/87	07/01/92	120	45	cc,ar nc
Madagascar	07/13/82	07/01/82-06/30/83	85	03/31/87	09/30/91	110	0	cc,ar st,nc
Romania	07/28/82	01/01/82-12/31/82	80	12/31/85	12/31/88	400	50	ar
Malawi	09/22/82	07/01/82-06/30/83	85	01/01/87	07/01/91	25	1	nc

Country	Agreed Minute Signed	Consolidation Period	Percent Consolidated	Repayment of Consolidated Debt[a] First	Repayment of Consolidated Debt[a] Last	Amount of Rescheduled Debt[b] (millions of $) Paris Club	Amount of Rescheduled Debt[b] (millions of $) U.S.	Remarks[c]
Senegal	11/29/82	07/01/82-06/30/83	85	09/30/87	03/31/92	$ 70	$ 3	nc
Uganda	12/01/82	07/01/82-06/30/83	90	12/31/87	06/30/92	20	1	nc
Costa Rica	01/11/83	07/01/82-12/31/83	85	09/30/87	03/31/92	110	25	ar,nc
Sudan	02/04/83	01/01/83-12/31/83	100	07/01/89	01/01/99	540	45	cc,ar,st pr,mi
Cuba	03/01/83	09/01/82-12/31/83	95	07/01/86	01/01/91	410	0	p,nc
Togo	04/12/83	01/01/83-12/31/83	90	12/31/88	06/30/93	140	1	cc,ar nc,pr
Zambia	05/16/83	01/01/83-12/31/83	90	12/31/88	06/30/93	210	50	ar,st nc
Romania	05/18/83	01/01/83-12/31/83	60	12/31/86	12/31/89	200	40	p,nc
Mexico	06/22/83	07/01/83-12/31/83	90	12/31/86	06/30/89	1,650	600	ar,p[e]
Cent. Afr. Republic	07/08/83	01/01/83-12/31/83	90	12/31/88	06/30/93	20	1	cc,st ar
Peru	07/26/83	05/01/83-04/30/84	90	04/30/87	10/31/91	580	145	nc
	and	05/01/84-04/30/85	[f]	04/30/88	10/31/92	[f]	[f]	imf
Ecuador	07/28/83	06/01/83-05/31/84	85	05/31/87	11/30/91	180	70	nc
Morocco	10/25/83	09/01/83-12/31/84	85	09/30/88	03/31/92	1,030	180	ar,nc
Malawi	10/27/83	07/01/83-06/30/84	85	01/01/88	07/01/92	20	1	nc

Country	Agreed Minute Signed	Consolidation Period	Percent Consolidated	Repayment of Consolidated Debt[a] First	Repayment of Consolidated Debt[a] Last	Amount of Rescheduled Debt[b] (millions of $) Paris Club	Amount of Rescheduled Debt[b] (millions of $) U.S.	Remarks[c]
Niger	11/14/83	10/01/83-09/31/84	90/60[g]	04/01/89	04/01/93	$ 30	$ 2	nc
Brazil	11/23/83	08/01/83-12/31/84	85	01/01/89	07/01/92	3,600	250	ar,nc
Zaire	12/20/83	01/01/84-12/31/84	95	12/31/89	06/30/95	900	145	cc,ar nc,pr,oa
Senegal	12/21/83	07/01/83-06/30/84	90	06/30/88	12/31/92	90	2	cc,nc
Liberia	12/22/83	07/01/83-06/30/84	90	06/30/88	12/31/92	20	10	cc,nc
Sierra Leone	02/08/84	01/01/84-12/31/84	90	12/31/89	12/31/94	10	0	cc,ar, pr,nc,oa
Madagascar	03/23/84	07/01/83-12/31/84	95	09/30/89	03/31/95	170	5	cc,ar, pr,nc,oa
Sudan	05/03/84	01/01/84-12/31/84	100	01/01/91	07/01/00	260	30	cc,pr, mi,oa
Ivory Coast	05/04/84	12/01/83-12/31/84	100/50[g]	12/31/88	06/30/93	310	25	
Yugoslavia	05/22/84	01/01/84-12/31/84	100	12/31/88	06/30/91	750	120	p
Peru	06/05/84	05/01/84-07/31/85	90	06/15/90	12/15/93	600	200	nc
Togo	06/06/84	01/01/84-04/30/85	95	02/28/90	08/31/94	140	2	pr,nc
Jamaica	07/16/84	01/01/84-03/31/85	100/50[g]	02/15/89	08/15/93	100	65	ar
Cuba	07/19/84	01/01/84-12/31/84	100	07/01/89	07/01/93	200	0	p

Country	*Agreed Minute Signed*	*Consolidation Period*	*Percent Consolidated*	*Repayment of Consolidated Debt*[a] *First*	*Last*	*Amount of Rescheduled Debt*[b] *(millions of $)* *Paris Club*	*U.S.*	*Remarks*[c]
Zambia	07/20/84	01/01/84-12/31/84	100	12/31/89	06/30/94	$ 200	$ 20	cc,ar, pr,oa
Ecuador	07/28/84	06/01/83-05/31/84	85	05/31/87	11/30/91	180	40	nc
Mozambique	10/25/84	07/01/84-06/30/85	95	06/30/90	12/31/95	350	10	ar,nc,oa
Niger	11/30/84	10/01/84-07/01/85	90/50[g]	11/01/90	05/01/95	25	2	nc
Liberia	12/17/84	07/01/84-06/30/85	90	06/30/90	12/31/94	15	5	nc,oa
Philippines	12/20/84	01/01/85-06/30/86	100/60[g]	03/15/91	09/15/95	1,280	375	ar,nc
Total						$26,990	$4,785	

[a] Made in semiannual installments in every case listed.

[b] Very rough approximations. In most cases, there were significant differences between the debtors' estimates and the creditors' estimates of arrears and payments falling due during the consolidation period. Even if the estimates were the same, there is no consensus on how to calculate the amount of debt relief. In some cases, the amount shown is total eligible debt. In others, the amount refers to consolidated debt only, or to everything except the portions to be paid according to the original schedules, or to the debt relief net of interest paid on rescheduled debt.

[c] ar = arrears rescheduled, including short-term arrears in some cases.
cc = contract cutoff date used in a previous rescheduling moved up.
imf = relief in subsequent consolidation periods linked to compliance with an IMF arrangement.
mi = moratorium interest capitalized.
nc = nonconsolidated debt rescheduled.
oa = offshore account established.
p = only principal rescheduled.
pr = previously rescheduled debt rescheduled.
st = short-term debt due in consolidation period rescheduled.

[d] Only arrears rescheduled.

[e] Only obligations of private-sector borrowers rescheduled.

[f] Percent rescheduled in the second consolidation was to be negotiated at a subsequent meeting. Instead, a completely new agreement was negotiated in June 1984.

[g] First percentage relates to principal payments and second to interest payments.

PUBLICATIONS OF THE INTERNATIONAL FINANCE SECTION

Notice to Contributors

The International Finance Section publishes at irregular intervals papers in four series: ESSAYS IN INTERNATIONAL FINANCE, PRINCETON STUDIES IN INTERNATIONAL FINANCE, SPECIAL PAPERS IN INTERNATIONAL ECONOMICS, and REPRINTS IN INTERNATIONAL FINANCE. ESSAYS and STUDIES are confined to subjects in international finance. SPECIAL PAPERS are surveys of the literature suitable for courses in colleges and universities.

An ESSAY should be a lucid exposition of a theme, accessible not only to the professional economist but to other interested readers. It should therefore avoid technical terms, should eschew mathematics and statistical tables (except when essential for an understanding of the text), and should rarely have footnotes.

A STUDY or SPECIAL PAPER may be more technical. It may include statistics and algebra and may have many footnotes. STUDIES and SPECIAL PAPERS may also be longer than ESSAYS; indeed, these two series are meant to accommodate manuscripts too long for journal articles and too short for books.

To facilitate prompt evaluation, please submit three copies of your manuscript. Retain one for your files. The manuscript should be typed on one side of 8½ by 11 strong white paper. All material should be double-spaced—text, excerpts, footnotes, tables, references, and figure legends. For more complete guidance, prospective contributors should send for the Section's style guide before preparing their manuscripts.

How to Obtain Publications

A mailing list is maintained for free distribution of all new publications to college, university, and public libraries and nongovernmental, nonprofit research institutions.

Individuals and organizations not qualifying for free distribution can obtain ESSAYS and REPRINTS as issued and announcements of new STUDIES and SPECIAL PAPERS by paying a fee of $12 (within U.S.) or $15 (outside U.S.) to cover the period January 1 through December 31, 1986. Alternatively, for $30 they can receive all publications automatically—SPECIAL PAPERS and STUDIES as well as ESSAYS and REPRINTS.

ESSAYS and REPRINTS can also be ordered from the Section at $2.50 per copy, and STUDIES and SPECIAL PAPERS at $4.50. Payment MUST be included with the order and MUST be made in U.S. dollars. PLEASE INCLUDE $1 FOR POSTAGE AND HANDLING. (These charges are waived on orders from persons or organizations in countries whose foreign-exchange regulations prohibit such remittances.) For airmail delivery outside U.S., Canada, and Mexico, there is an additional charge of $1.

All manuscripts, correspondence, and orders should be addressed to:

International Finance Section
Department of Economics, Dickinson Hall
Princeton University
Princeton, New Jersey 08544

Subscribers should notify the Section promptly of a change of address, giving the old address as well as the new one.

List of Recent Publications

Some earlier issues are still in print. Write the Section for information.

ESSAYS IN INTERNATIONAL FINANCE

130. Franco Modigliani and Tommaso Padoa-Schioppa, *The Management of an Open Economy with "100% Plus" Wage Indexation.* (Dec. 1978)
131. H. Robert Heller and Malcolm Knight, *Reserve-Currency Preferences of Central Banks.* (Dec. 1978)
132. Robert Triffin, *Gold and the Dollar Crisis: Yesterday and Tomorrow.* (Dec. 1978)
133. Herbert G. Grubel, *A Proposal for the Establishment of an International Deposit Insurance Corporation.* (July 1979)
134. Bertil Ohlin, *Some Insufficiencies in the Theories of International Economic Relations.* (Sept. 1979)
135. Frank A. Southard, Jr., *The Evolution of the International Monetary Fund.* (Dec. 1979)
136. Niels Thygesen, *Exchange-Rate Experiences and Policies of Small Countries: Some European Examples in the 1970s.* (Dec. 1979)
137. Robert M. Dunn, Jr., *Exchange Rates, Payments Adjustments, and OPEC: Why Oil Deficits Persist.* (Dec. 1979)
138. Tom de Vries, *On the Meaning and Future of the European Monetary System.* (Sept. 1980)
139. Deepak Lal, *A Liberal International Economic Order: The International Monetary System and Economic Development.* (Oct. 1980)
140. Pieter Korteweg, *Exchange-Rate Policy, Monetary Policy, and Real Exchange-Rate Variability.* (Dec. 1980)
141. Bela Balassa, *The Process of Industrial Development and Alternative Development Strategies.* (Dec. 1980)
142. Benjamin J. Cohen, *The European Monetary System: An Outsider's View.* (June 1981)
143. Marina v. N. Whitman, *International Trade and Investment: Two Perspectives.* (July 1981)
144. Sidney Dell, *On Being Grandmotherly: The Evolution of IMF Conditionality.* (Oct. 1981)
145. Ronald I. McKinnon and Donald J. Mathieson, *How to Manage a Repressed Economy.* (Dec. 1981)

*146. Bahram Nowzad, *The IMF and Its Critics.* (Dec. 1981)

147. Edmar Lisboa Bacha and Carlos F. Díaz Alejandro, *International Financial Intermediation: A Long and Tropical View.* (May 1982)
148. Alan A. Rabin and Leland B. Yeager, *Monetary Approaches to the Balance of Payments and Exchange Rates.* (Nov. 1982)
149. C. Fred Bergsten, Rudiger Dornbusch, Jacob A. Frenkel, Steven W. Kohlhagen, Luigi Spaventa, and Thomas D. Willett, *From Rambouillet to Versailles: A Symposium.* (Dec. 1982)

*Out of print. Available on demand in xerographic paperback or library-bound copies from University Microfilms International, Box 1467, Ann Arbor, Michigan 48106, United States, and 30-32 Mortimer St., London, WIN 7RA, England. Paperback reprints are usually $20. Microfilm of all Essays by year is also available from University Microfilms. Photocopied sheets of out-of-print titles are available on demand from the Section at $6 per Essay and $8 per Study or Special Paper.

150. Robert E. Baldwin, *The Inefficacy of Trade Policy*. (Dec. 1982)
151. Jack Guttentag and Richard Herring, *The Lender-of-Last Resort Function in an International Context*. (May 1983)
152. G. K. Helleiner, *The IMF and Africa in the 1980s*. (July 1983)
153. Rachel McCulloch, *Unexpected Real Consequences of Floating Exchange Rates*. (Aug. 1983)
154. Robert M. Dunn, Jr., *The Many Disappointments of Floating Exchange Rates*. (Dec. 1983)
155. Stephen Marris, *Managing the World Economy: Will We Ever Learn?* (Oct. 1984)
156. Sebastian Edwards, *The Order of Liberalization of the External Sector in Developing Countries*. (Dec. 1984)
157. Wilfred J. Ethier and Richard C. Marston, eds., with Kindleberger, Guttentag and Herring, Wallich, Henderson, and Hinshaw, *International Financial Markets and Capital Movements: A Symposium in Honor of Arthur I. Bloomfield*. (Sept. 1985)
158. Charles E. Dumas, *The Effects of Government Deficits: A Comparative Analysis of Crowding Out*. (Oct. 1985)
159. Jeffrey A. Frankel, *Six Possible Meanings of "Overvaluation": The 1981-85 Dollar*. (Dec. 1985)
160. Stanley W. Black, *Learning from Adversity: Policy Responses to Two Oil Shocks*. (Dec. 1985)
161. Alexis Rieffel, *The Role of the Paris Club in Managing Debt Problems*. (Dec. 1985)

PRINCETON STUDIES IN INTERNATIONAL FINANCE

44. Clas Wihlborg, *Currency Risks in International Financial Markets*. (Dec. 1978)
45. Ian M. Drummond, *London, Washington, and the Management of the Franc, 1936-39*. (Nov. 1979)
46. Susan Howson, *Sterling's Managed Float: The Operations of the Exchange Equalisation Account, 1932-39*. (Nov. 1980)
47. Jonathan Eaton and Mark Gersovitz, *Poor Country Borrowing in Private Financial Markets and the Repudiation Issue*. (June 1981)
48. Barry J. Eichengreen, *Sterling and the Tariff, 1929-32*. (Sept. 1981)
49. Peter Bernholz, *Flexible Exchange Rates in Historical Perspective*. (July 1982)
50. Victor Argy, *Exchange-Rate Management in Theory and Practice*. (Oct. 1982)
51. Paul Wonnacott, *U.S. Intervention in the Exchange Market for DM, 1977-80*. (Dec. 1982)
52. Irving B. Kravis and Robert E. Lipsey, *Toward an Explanation of National Price Levels*. (Nov. 1983)
53. Avraham Ben-Bassat, *Reserve-Currency Diversification and the Substitution Account*. (March 1984)

*54. Jeffrey Sachs, *Theoretical Issues in International Borrowing*. (July 1984)

55. Marsha R. Shelburn, *Rules for Regulating Intervention under a Managed Float*. (Dec. 1984)
56. Paul De Grauwe, Marc Janssens, and Hilde Leliaert, *Real-Exchange-Rate Variability from 1920 to 1926 and 1973 to 1982*. (Sept. 1985)

8. Jagdish Bhagwati, *The Theory and Practice of Commercial Policy: Departures from Unified Exchange Rates*. (Jan. 1968)
*9. Marina von Neumann Whitman, *Policies for Internal and External Balance*. (Dec. 1970)
10. Richard E. Caves, *International Trade, International Investment, and Imperfect Markets*. (Nov. 1974)
*11. Edward Tower and Thomas D. Willett, *The Theory of Optimum Currency Areas and Exchange-Rate Flexibility*. (May 1976)
*12. Ronald W. Jones, *"Two-ness" in Trade Theory: Costs and Benefits*. (April 1977)
13. Louka T. Katseli-Papaefstratiou, *The Reemergence of the Purchasing Power Parity Doctrine in the 1970s*. (Dec. 1979)
*14. Morris Goldstein, *Have Flexible Exchange Rates Handicapped Macroeconomic Policy?* (June 1980)
15. Gene M. Grossman and J. David Richardson, *Strategic Trade Policy: A Survey of Issues and Early Analysis*. (April 1985)

REPRINTS IN INTERNATIONAL FINANCE

18. Peter B. Kenen, *Floats, Glides and Indicators: A Comparison of Methods for Changing Exchange Rates*. [Reprinted from *Journal of International Economics*, 5 (May 1975).] (June 1975)
19. Polly R. Allen and Peter B. Kenen, *The Balance of Payments, Exchange Rates, and Economic Policy: A Survey and Synthesis of Recent Developments*. [Reprinted from Center of Planning and Economic Research, Occasional Paper 33, Athens, Greece, 1978.] (April 1979)
20. William H. Branson, *Asset Markets and Relative Prices in Exchange Rate Determination*. [Reprinted from *Sozialwissenschaftliche Annalen*, Vol. 1, 1977.] (June 1980)
21. Peter B. Kenen, *The Analytics of a Substitution Account*. [Reprinted from *Banca Nazionale del Lavoro Quarterly Review*, No. 139 (Dec. 1981).] (Dec. 1981)
22. Jorge Braga de Macedo, *Exchange Rate Behavior with Currency Inconvertibility*. [Reprinted from *Journal of International Economics*, 12 (Feb. 1982).] (Sept. 1982)
23. Peter B. Kenen, *Use of the SDR to Supplement or Substitute for Other Means of Finance*. [Reprinted from George M. von Furstenberg, ed., *International Money and Credit: The Policy Roles*, Washington, IMF, 1983, Chap. 7.] (Dec. 1983)